Silence and Honey Cakes

Rowan Williams

Silence
and
Honey
Cakes

The wisdom
of the desert

Medio
Media

LION

To Fra Enzo and the Community of Bose

Text by Rowan Williams
Copyright © 2003 Medio Media
Illustrations by Earle Backen, Kate McDonnell
Leigh Hurlock and Eric Drewery

Published by Lion Books
an imprint of
Lion Hudson plc
Wilkinson House, Jordan Hill Road,
Oxford OX2 8DR, England
www.lionhudson.com/lion

ISBN 978 0 7459 5170 6 (print)
ISBN 978 0 7459 5822 4 (epub)
ISBN 978 0 7459 5821 7 (Kindle)

First hardback edition 2003
This edition 2004

A catalogue record for this book is available
from the British Library

Printed and bound in the UK, April 2016, LH26

Contents

Introduction

The growth and expansion of Christian monasticism in the deserts of Egypt from the mid third century is an extraordinary phenomenon. I use the present tense here because, as Rowan Williams illustrates in his exposition of the wisdom of this movement, it is a phenomenon that is still with us. We may not be able to understand it fully, but if its power to fascinate captures even those who do not share the faith of the desert fathers and mothers, then even the attempt to understand it will enrich and stimulate our spiritual awareness. These monastic oddballs of an unimaginably different and ancient world may indeed hold a secret for our modern world that no economist, sociologist, politician or religious leader can match. The desert wisdom teaches rather than preaches. Its authority is experiential not theoretical. The upshot of this is a phenomenon that many modern people, disenchanted with religious institutionalism, will find unusual – a religious group that is grasped by the experience of God as absolute, uncompromising in its longing to be united with it and yet remaining humorous, humble and, above all, not condemning those of other beliefs or practice.

As Rowan Williams elegantly describes, the teachers of the desert were striking *individuals*. They loved and sought solitude. But they were also *persons* held in a network of realistic relationships in community. Why they began, when they did, to leave the towns and villages of the fertile inhabited regions of the Nile delta and settle, at first, in the inhospitable 'exterior desert' is partly due to the persecution of Christians by Decius. But even after the persecution subsided, the monks remained. Furthermore they began to plunge deeper into the 'full desert' as they called it. They renounced the socio-economic world and family life as completely as Indian sannyasis. However, their collected sayings – the substance of the teaching that has descended to us – show it was not a misanthropy or hatred of the world. It was renunciation *not* rejection; a passion for the absolute but not intolerance or fundamentalism; and above all not self-righteousness. They knew how easy it is for religious people to fall into the self-contradictory sin of pride, and the monks of the desert feared this pitfall more than any other. This was why they kept seeking deeper desert, to escape the fame that began early on to attach itself to them. They were not very well-adjusted individuals if we look at them from the standards of the worldly success they had abandoned. Yet if we judge them by what they believed, they had an authenticity and simplicity about them that still touches our hearts and wins our admiration.

They were fighters not escapees, pilgrims not tourists. If this phenomenon erupted where it did it is perhaps because religion and geography are not unaligned. In no other country does the desert come so close to the populated world. It is not an abstract idea as the 'bush' or the 'wilderness' can be to modern people. The desert is always present to the Egyptian in the dramatic contrast between the rich black soil of the Nile valley and the sterile sand of the desert. Herodotus was the first to remark on the intensely religious nature of the Egyptian people for whom religious truth was both the commonest and the highest of all values. This geography and religious passion had earlier been the ancient setting of the conflict between Osiris and Horus, the Egyptian gods of life, and Seth the god of opposition and negation. The desert fathers and mothers were fighting the ancient fight – whose main scene of operation is the human heart – but with the new weapon of their faith in the power and reality of Christ.

Following their legendary pioneer, St Antony, they plunged further and further into the desert and formed the eremitical centres of Nitria, the Cells and Scetis. By the end of the fourth century the old men were grumbling about there being too many monks, 5000 in Nitria alone it was estimated and 600 in the even remoter Cells. Pilgrims, seekers and tourists came, some just to bug them, others to sit seriously at their feet and continue the lineage. One of these visitors, who stayed twenty years, was a young man from present-day Romania called John Cassian. Early in the fifth century he returned to Europe and established a monastic community for men and women in Marseilles. The ideal of desert monasticism had already reached as far as the west coast of Ireland. But it was an influence largely dependent on the already famous collections of the 'sound bites' of the fathers' sayings, with their striking similarity at times to Zen stories, and what there was of direct personal experience. Cassian agreed to a request by a local bishop anxious about the unruliness of the monastic movement – still an untamed lay movement – to compose a more methodical presentation of the teachings of the desert wisdom. His great work the *Conferences of the Fathers* was the result. A generation later St Benedict, who had himself begun his monastic life on the Desert model, recommended in his Rule that the Conferences should be read every day at mealtimes. By these stages and connections the spiritual pioneers of the Egyptian desert entered deeply into the mind and culture of western society.

The monasticism they thus inspired and that Benedict organized and adapted to western conditions became a major shaping force in European civilization. Through the Dark Ages that followed the collapse of Rome as the sole super-power, the Rule of Benedict inspired and sustained an alternative form of life. It was a life in hard-working, economically self-sufficient communities conscious of their responsibilities to the world around them but practising a gospel form of the radical detachment exemplified by the desert fathers. The Benedictine life, about which Rowan Williams has also taught, was itself a civilizing force because it worked through the contagious power of example rather than by the force of imposing uniformity. What was so attractive and influential about the Benedictine lifestyle? Surely its understanding of the human need for peace in any lifestyle that promises sustainable growth in personal development. Holiness – or wholeness as people prefer to say today – requires a degree of inner and outer peace that respects the at times conflicting, though not contradictory, demands of body, mind and spirit. The first requirement for this peace or harmony is order in human living and a right use of time. This is what Benedict so brilliantly and calmly concentrates on – a community that respects differences but controls the ego while managing time realistically around the central priority of prayer.

Maybe the Rule 'saved civilization' but it is still, according to Benedict himself, just a beginning in the spiritual journey. For him the ideal of the desert father was never far from sight. Externally this might mean that after years in the monastery the monk would move into a form of solitude. Interiorly it should mean that prayer becomes increasingly 'pure'. That means that it is more centred in and characterized by the silence of the heart and less in the images and concepts of mental prayer or in external ritual. Western monasticism institutionally forgot this. Inevitably, then, the institution ossified and its considerable political and economic influence collapsed. Not one English monastic community resisted its dissolution and appropriation by the state in the sixteenth century. Today the monastic movement continues although often without quite knowing why, or how they should relate to the wider world. The heady days of the Egyptian desert are still studied but seem very archaic to most monks. Many monasteries have closed or are contracting for lack of vocations. Yet the greater wonder is that they are still there, testifying sometimes to their own amazement to the inextinguishable flame of the monastic archetype in the human psyche that Benedict summarized as 'seeking God'.

In 1969 John Main, an Irish Benedictine, was going through a difficult chapter in his own life. There had been conflict in his community in London and he had been sent to a monastery in the United States. He became headmaster of the school and struggled with the cultural revolution underway but also learned from it. When a young student, like a modern-day Cassian, visited and asked John Main for an introduction to Christian mysticism the *Conferences of the Fathers* proved their mysterious and enduring power of inspiration. This led John Main to read Cassian again, no longer to pass exams but to answer questions about contemporary spiritual hunger. In the Tenth Conference, *On Prayer*, he came across the radiant nucleus of desert spirituality, a forgotten key to the prayer of the heart. In this conference Cassian addresses the practice of prayer and its practical difficulties, the greatest of which and root of them all is distraction. The remedy he advises is the simple practice of meditation in the faith-filled repetition of a single *formula* or mantra. Main realized this was a pearl of spiritual teaching. More than a *lectio* or reading of scripture, more than a cultivation of inner quietness, he saw it was a spiritual discipline, an ascesis of the kind necessary to effect serious and sustainable change in the person praying. His own experience of learning meditation in Asia before he became a monk had helped him to recognize the specific value and meaning of Cassian's recommendation and then to pick up the thread of this teaching throughout the Christian tradition.

Thus the seed of The World Community for Christian Meditation was planted. Or rather thus it fell from the fertile seedbed of desert wisdom. Just as an ancient desert father attracted disciples just by sitting in meditation, so around the teaching of John Main a community has formed. The pattern is ever the same – it is this sameness that makes the desert wisdom so ever fresh and useful to us. But the form it takes today is different. A more than local phenomenon has resulted. There are no more Nitrias and Scetis on the same scale. But through the practice of Christian meditation the desert wisdom has led to a global community reflecting the 'new holiness' of the modern world. The new monks of the Christian world have a new look. Some live in traditional monasteries but the majority do not. Many are integrating what previously seemed impossible to reconcile – deep spiritual practice and conjugal love, solitude and social responsibility.

Contemporary holiness needs to acknowledge the expansion of the human mind into a multi-cultural and indeed multi-faith communion. And this is the enormous challenge to Christianity today. Either it grows into the future with the courage and faith showed by the ancient monks as they penetrated further and further into the heart of the desert to find the true God, renouncing the god of their imagining. Or – what is the alternative? Only to bury its head in the sand. Deeper faith or ever more superficial fundamentalism is the constant choice of religion – as basic as the struggle between Osiris and Seth or that of the desert fathers with their own fears and desires. As Rowan Williams shows it is also our personal choice and struggle every day.

What led Rowan Williams into friendship with The World Community for Christian Meditation and to his support for it also led to his giving the 2001 John Main Seminar in Sydney, Australia. The Seminar then led to this book which is an important contribution to the renewal and expansion of the Christian mind today. It reflects his own prophetic perception that one thing always leads to another and that if we trace this sequence back to its origins we have found the direction we should be moving in.

Laurence Freeman OSB
Director of The World Community for Christian Meditation

www.wccm.org

Preface

The invitation to lead the John Main Seminar for 2001 in Sydney came as a great surprise and delight, and I want to express the warmest of thanks to The World Community for Christian Meditation for this opportunity. Fr Laurence Freeman helped and supported me in many ways before and during this event, and I owe him a great debt of gratitude for his assistance in transcribing and editing the talks in such a way that I was able to use them as the basis for this complete written version. What follows is therefore not a direct transcript of what was said – except for the question and answer session printed as an appendix, which has been only very slightly revised for publication. The bulk of the text follows the order and subject matter of the talks, but expands some points and introduces a few broader references. However, I hope it retains some of the flavour of the spoken word – and if it does so, that is largely due to Fr Laurence's help in the early stages of moving from the spoken word to the page.

My first serious acquaintance with the monastic literature of the desert came by way of friendship with one of the greatest contemporary scholars and expositors of the tradition, Sister Benedicta Ward, at the time when she was first engaged in translating the material for her classic version of the most significant text of the literature, *The Sayings of the Desert Fathers*.[1] Like everyone else who has worked in this area, I owe her a lasting and incalculable debt.

Almost every time I have tried to write a book, I have discovered in the last stages of composition that someone else is about to publish a better one on more or less the same subject. This is a pity for me, but very helpful for everyone else. On this occasion the book in question is John Chryssavgis's study, *In the Heart of the Desert:*

The Spirituality of the Desert Fathers and Mothers.[2] I was delighted to be able to see an advance copy of this and to include a couple of quotations from what will undoubtedly be a work of lasting value.

The final work on my text was done during a stay at the Monastery of Bose in Northern Italy. The welcome of the community was quite unforgettable, and it is a pleasure to dedicate this book to a group of men and women who are such a sign of the continuing vitality of the contemplative life in a thoroughly contemporary mode.

Two closing observations. To speak in Australia about the desert tradition had and has a special resonance: this is a country with the desert at its heart, a desert that it has only begun to explore spiritually. The strong sense at the 2001 seminar of an impulse in the Australian churches to engage more seriously with this exploration was a profound and moving thing for all those present from other countries. And of course, to speak of the desert tradition at an event commemorating John Main had its own appropriateness, given that Fr John was one of those who most effectively put the tradition to work in our own day. The roots of his distinctive spirituality lie deep in the fourth and fifth centuries, especially in the work of that great expositor of the desert world, John Cassian. The World Community which continues his mission is for me, as for many throughout the world, a taste of what a committedly contemplative church might look and feel like, with its intense fidelity to shared silence as well as to shared belief and experience. This little book is meant as a modest contribution to the discovery of a church renewed in contemplation across the cultural frontiers of our world.

Introductory Note on Sources

The sayings and stories associated with the first generations of Christian monks and nuns in the Egyptian desert were evidently being collected orally during or soon after their lifetimes. But the development of written collections took longer, and the written material we have inevitably shows signs of editing and signs of concern about issues that may not have been that important in the 'real time' of the stories, and so on. The generations most liberally represented in the oldest collections of sayings are those who flourished between about 350 and about 450 – though the most influential figure, Antony the Great, was most active just before this period and died at the age of 105 in 356.

Many of the figures remembered in the tradition therefore lived through years of acute crisis in the Egyptian monastic world. Around 400, the Egyptian communities – and their friends and supporters elsewhere – were bitterly divided over theological matters. The detail is hard to pin down objectively at times, since most reports are heavily slanted, but it was broadly about the influence of speculative and philosophical ideas on theology – especially those ideas associated with the great third-century Alexandrian teacher Origen, who was brilliant but theologically suspect. In particular, there was concern as to whether his teaching, or teachings derived from it, encouraged a false attitude to the human body (and thus to the incarnation of God in Jesus Christ). Traces of this conflict can be found here and there in the literature. Archbishop Theophilus, a fierce opponent of the Origenist party, is sometimes presented in a rather ambivalent light. He was responsible for the exile of several leading ascetics from Egypt, and those who later settled in Palestine were certainly among those who helped to give shape to the tradition of the sayings as we have them. But equally there is a certain lukewarmness in the presentation of a figure like Evagrius, the foremost theologian of the Origenist group and an immense influence on many later figures. It is as if the literature is trying to pick its way through explosive territory. Stories about dramatic physical manifestations of God's grace in prayer – the flames shooting from the raised hands of a monk praising God in solitude – may reflect a concern to steer away from too much suspicion of the material world. But again, stories centring on the hard work of daily and unrewarding labour may register a caution against looking for too much visible drama. And the various ways in which 'thoughts' – really a technical term for distracting or even obsessive mental activity – are discussed often indicates a familiarity with the vocabulary of Evagrius's circle.

One could go on spotting these telltale signs of a context more complicated than the surface suggests, but the point is that by the time the major early collections had been assembled in something like their present form – in the first half of the fifth century probably – they were being used as fundamentally coherent guides to the life of prayer and asceticism. There are obvious differences of emphasis, and sometimes more than that, but these were evidently seen as part of a discipline that did not seek to produce lifeless uniformity. As the following pages will, I hope, make clear, there was a healthy readiness to live with the variety of perspectives and to respect the living diversity of monastic discipline. It is this which makes the sayings traditions so endlessly intriguing and stretching – and it is this which has ensured their survival and constant 'recycling' across the centuries.

The two great early collections in Greek, the 'Alphabetical' and the 'Anonymous', are the source for practically everything discussed here; the former tells stories associated with specific people from the first monastic generations, the latter groups sayings and stories by subject (and suggests incidentally what other evidence confirms, that there were several stories that could attach themselves to different names or to no name at all). Both collections have been translated in their entirety by Sister Benedicta Ward in a most accessible form. My translations in this book owe a great deal to hers, as will be clear, but I have not always followed the same choice of idiom.

Life, Death and Neighbours

'Our life and our death is with our neighbour. If we win our brother, we win God. If we cause our brother to stumble, we have sinned against Christ.'

One thing that comes out very clearly from any reading of the great monastic writers of the fourth and fifth centuries is the impossibility of thinking about contemplation or meditation or 'spiritual life' in abstraction from the actual business of living in the Body of Christ, living in concrete community. The life of intimacy with God in contemplation is both the fruit and the course of a renewed style of living together. So in these reflections on the legacy of the desert monastics, I hope to look at how they saw the whole of this life together and to look at where they thought contemplation came from and where it led to. I believe that if we can do this, we shall learn something of where we in turn may look for the wellsprings of renewal in our community as Christians seeking God in prayer and common life. We are always faced with the danger of trying to think about this odd thing called 'spiritual life' as if it were a matter we could deal with in isolation, and it is often very attractive to attempt this, simply because the facts of human life together are normally so messy, so unpromising and unedifying. Other people in their actual material reality do make things a lot more difficult, when what we *think* we want is spirituality – the cultivation of a sensitive and rewarding relationship with eternal truth and love. And this is where the desert monastics have an uncompromising message for us: a relationship with eternal truth and love simply doesn't happen unless we mend our relations with Tom, Dick and Harriet. The actual substance of our relationship with eternal truth and love is bound up with how we manage the proximity of these human neighbours.

At first sight, it seems as though the monastic movement was all about avoiding the compromises that the presence of other human beings entailed. We'll be looking later on at the very common language, which we encounter in the writings of the desert, of 'fleeing' from other people and the impulse of monasticism had a lot to do with the worry felt by increasing numbers of Christians that the church of their day was becoming corrupt and secularized. The early monks and nuns moved off into the communities of the desert because they weren't convinced that the church in its 'ordinary' manifestations showed with any clarity what the church was supposed to be about; they wanted to find out what the church really was – which is another way of saying that they wanted to find out what humanity really was when it was in touch with God through Jesus Christ. What we have in the literature associated with the early generations of desert ascetics is their reporting back from the 'laboratory of the Spirit' not only about how prayer is to be experienced but about how humanity is to be understood – about life, death and neighbours.

The phrase derives from a saying of Antony the Great, the earliest and most influential of Christian monastic teachers:

Our life and our death is with our neighbour. If we win our brother, we win God. If we cause our brother to stumble, we have sinned against Christ.[1]

We can compare this with some material from a generation later, which comes to us under the name of Moses the Black – a figure we shall meet again. He was one of the most vivid personalities of the early monastic world, a rather larger-than-life character whose teaching and sometimes slightly anarchic example appear in many stories. A converted Ethiopian highwayman (physically as well as in other ways larger than life), his burial place is still shown to visitors near the monastery of Baramous in the desert west of Cairo – which is one small sign of the extraordinary continuity to be experienced at such sites. Moses is credited with a series of summary proverb-like sayings about the monastic life, which were written for another great teacher, Abba Poemen. One of these sayings seems to pick up the language of Antony, yet to give it a twist that is at first sight very puzzling. 'The monk,' says Moses, 'must die to his neighbour and never judge him at all in any way whatever.'[2] If our life and our death are with the neighbour, this spells out something of what our 'death' to the neighbour might mean: it is to renounce the power of judgment over someone else – a task hard enough indeed to merit being described as death. The basis of this is elaborated in another of the Moses sayings. In reply to a brother who wants to know what it means to 'think in your heart that you are a sinner', which is defined as another of the essentials of the monastic life, Moses says, 'If you are occupied with your own faults, you have no time to see those of your neighbour.'[3]

We begin to see here the cluster of ideas generated by the apparently simple words of Antony. Living in a Christian way with the neighbour, so that the neighbour is 'won' – i.e. converted, brought into saving relation with Jesus Christ – involves my 'death'. I must die to myself, a self understood as the solid possessor of virtues and gifts, entitled to pronounce on the neighbour's spiritual condition. My own awareness of my failure and weakness is indispensable to my communicating the gospel to my neighbour. I put the neighbour in touch with God by a particular kind of detachment from him or her. And, the desert writers insist, this is absolutely basic for our growth in the life of grace. Here is a saying under the name of John the Dwarf:

'You don't build a house by starting with the roof and working down. You start with the foundation.'
    They said, 'What does that mean?'
    He said, 'The foundation is our neighbour whom we must win. The neighbour is where we start. Every commandment of Christ depends on this.'[4]

Everything begins with this vision and hope of putting the neighbour in touch with God in Christ. On this the rest of our Christian life depends, and it entails facing the death of a particular kind of picture of myself. If I fail to put someone in touch with God, I face another sort of death, the death of my relation with Christ, because failing to 'win' the neighbour is to stand in the way of Christ, to block Christ's urgent will to communicate with all.

The desert monastics are keenly interested in diagnosing what sort of things get in the way here, what things count as blocking someone else's relation with Christ. They seem very well aware that one of the great temptations of religious living is the urge to intrude between God and other people. We love to think that we know more of God than others; we find it comfortable and comforting to try and control the access of others to God. Jesus himself speaks bluntly about this when he describes the religious enthusiasts of his day shutting the door of the Kingdom in the face of others: 'You do not enter yourselves, and when others try to enter, you stop them' (Matthew 23:13). And he goes on to describe how such people exert themselves to gain even one convert, but because they are only trying to make others in their own image, they make them twice as worthy of condemnation as themselves. The desert teachers are well aware that by fleeing to the isolation of prayerful communities they do not automatically leave behind this deep-rooted longing to manage the access of other people to God. This is why they insist upon an ever-greater honesty about the self; this is why the 'manifesting of thoughts' to a senior brother or sister becomes so crucial – because everyone is drawn almost irresistibly back towards this urge to manage.

One of the most frequent ways in which this becomes visible, they suggest, is *inattention*, the failure to see what is truly there in front of us – because our own vision is clouded by self-obsession or self-satisfaction. There are several variants of a story in which some young monk goes in despair to one of the great 'old men' to say that he has consulted an elder about his temptations and been told to do severe and intolerable penance, then the old man tells the younger one to return to his first counsellor and tell him that he has not paid proper attention to the need of the novice. If we don't really know how to attend to the reality that is our own inner turmoil, we shall fail in responding to the needs of someone else. And the desert literature suggests pretty consistently that excessive harshness – readiness to judge and prescribe – normally has its roots in that kind of inattention to ourselves. Abba Joseph responds to the invitation to join in condemning someone by saying, 'Who am I?' And the phrase might suggest not just 'Who am I to be judging?' but 'How can I pass judgment when I don't know the full truth about myself?'[5]

Among the longest collections of sayings attributed to

particular desert fathers are those around the names of Macarius the Great and Poemen (granted that 'Poemen', 'the shepherd', may be a name concealing several different figures), and these collections have in common an exceptional number of sayings on the subject of the dangers of harshness and self-satisfaction. Of Macarius, we read, in an unforgettable image, that 'he became like a God on earth' because when he saw the sins of the brothers, he would 'cover' them, just as God casts his protection over the world.[6] Informed of a self-confident monk whose counsel has depressed others, the elderly Macarius pays a visit:

When he was alone with him, Macarius asked, 'How are things going with you?' Theopemptus replied, 'Thanks to your prayers, all is well.' The old man asked, 'Do you not have to battle with your fantasies?' He answered, 'No, up to now all is well.' He was afraid to admit anything. But the old man said to him, 'I have lived for many years as an ascetic and everyone sings my praises, but despite my age, I still have trouble with sexual fantasies.' Theopemptus said, 'Well, it is the same with me, to tell the truth.' And the old man went on admitting, one by one, all the other fantasies that caused him to struggle, until he had brought Theopemptus to admit all of them himself. Then he said, 'What do you do about fasting?' 'Nothing till the ninth hour,' Theopemptus replied. 'Fast till evening and take some exercise,' said Macarius. 'Go over the words of the gospel and the rest of Scripture. And if an alien thought arises within you, don't look down but up: the Lord will come to your help.'[7]

Self-satisfaction is dealt with not by confrontation or condemnation but by the quiet personal exposure of failure in such a way as to prompt the same truthfulness in someone

27

else: the neighbour is won, or converted, by Macarius's 'death' to any hint of superiority in his vision of himself. He has nothing to defend, and he preaches the gospel by simple identification with the condition of another, a condition they cannot themselves face honestly. How tempting to go in and say, 'I know you suffer these temptations.' Macarius refuses this easy way and goes instead by the way of 'death to the neighbour', refusing to judge and exposing himself to judgment.

But we can find something like the opposite extreme in the stories as well. What about those who judge themselves too harshly? Abba Poemen is confronted with a brother who admits to having committed a great sin and wants to do three years' penance.

The old man said, 'That's a lot.' The brother said, 'What about one year?' The old man said, 'That's still quite a lot.' Some other people suggested forty days; Poemen said, 'That's a lot too.' And he said, 'What I think is that if someone repents with all their heart and intends never to commit the sin again, perhaps God will be satisfied with only three days.'[8]

The point of leading someone to confront their weakness and need is not to enforce discipline or cement patterns of spiritual superiority and inferiority. Whether it is a matter of persuading someone to admit what they have never admitted or of helping them to face mercifully what they have admitted, the goal is reconciliation with God by way of this combination of truth and mercy. A harsh judgment of others can lead to despair; several stories[9] turn on this, as we have already seen, when monks resort in fear or self-loathing to one of the great old men after receiving rough treatment from a less experienced elder. The fundamental need as far

as the counsellor is concerned is first of all to put themsel[ves]
on the level of the one who has sinned, to heal by solidarity
not condemnation. Hence stories like that of Moses:

*There was a brother at Scetis who had committed a fault. So they
called a meeting and invited Abba Moses. He refused to go. The
priest sent someone to say to him, 'They're all waiting for you.'
So Moses got up and set off; he took a leaky jug and filled it with
water and took it with him. The others came out to meet him and
said, 'What is this, Father?' The old man said to them, 'My sins
run out behind me and I cannot see them, yet here I am coming
to sit in judgment on the mistakes of somebody else.' When they
heard this, they called off the meeting.*[10]

An anonymous variant portrays one of the old men at the
same kind of meeting (how wonderfully recognizable is that
response – someone had committed a fault, so they called a
meeting!) getting up and leaving when sentence is passed.
'Where are you going, Father?' they ask. 'I have just been
condemned,' he replies.[11] And there is a similar portrayal of
Abba Bessarion:

*A brother who had sinned was turned out of the church by the
priest; Abba Bessarion got up and followed him out; he said,
'I too am a sinner.'*[12]

Macarius, as we have heard, was like a God in Scetis: he hid
what he saw as if he had not seen it, says the narrative.[13]

*A brother questioned Abba Poemen saying, 'If I see my brother
sinning, should I hide the fact?' The old man said, 'At the
moment when we hide a brother's fault, God hides our own.*

is written:

Some on... n came to see Abba Poemen and said to him, 'We
see some of the brothers falling asleep during divine worship.
Should we wake them up?' He said, 'As for me, when I see a
brother who is falling asleep during the Office, I lay his head on
my knees and let him rest.'[15]

We can be deceived into thinking that the desert monks and
nuns – at least those quoted here – are somehow indifferent
to sin, or that their notion of relation to one another is a
matter of bland acceptance. But they are not contemporary
exponents of some sort of 'I'm OK, you're OK' method. They
actually believe that sin is immensely serious and that
separation from God is a real possibility; if you define the
purpose of your life, a costly, boring, difficult life in physically
harsh conditions, as 'winning your neighbour', you may
reasonably be expected to believe that it is a tough and
serious business, in which success isn't guaranteed. But they
also take for granted that the only way in which you know
the seriousness of separation from God is in your own
experience of yourself. Moses writes to Poemen, 'If you have
sin enough in your own life and your own home, you have no
need to go searching for it elsewhere.' And, more graphically,
from Moses again, 'If you have a corpse laid out in your own
front room, you won't have leisure to go to a neighbour's
funeral.'[16] This is not about minimizing sin; it is about
learning how to recognize it from seeing the cost in yourself.
If it can't be addressed by you in terms of your own needs, it

can't be addressed anywhere – however seductive it is to say, 'I know how to deal with this problem in your life – and never mind about mine.'

The inattention and harshness that shows we have not grasped this is for so many of the desert monks and nuns the major way in which we fail in winning the neighbour. Poemen goes so far as to say that it is the one thing about which we can justly get angry with each other.

A brother asked Abba Poemen, 'What does it mean to be angry with your brother without a cause? [The reference is obviously to Matthew 5:21ff.]. He said, 'If your brother hurts you by his arrogance and you are angry with him because of this, that is getting angry without a cause. If he pulls out your right eye and cuts off your right hand and you get angry with him, that is getting angry without a cause. But if he cuts you off from God – then you have every right to be angry with him.'[17]

To assume the right to judge, or to assume that you have arrived at a settled spiritual maturity which entitles you to prescribe confidently at a distance for another's sickness is in fact to leave them without the therapy they need for their souls; it is to cut them off from God, to leave them in their spiritual slavery – while reinforcing your own slavery. Neither you nor they have access to life. As in the words of Jesus, you have shut up heaven for others and for yourself. But the plain acknowledgment of your solidarity in need and failure opens a door: it shows that it is possible to live in the truth and to go forward in hope. It is in such a moment that God gives himself through you, and you become by God's gift a means of connecting another with God. You have done the job you were created to do.

If we ask how this literature contributes to any kind of contemporary understanding of Christian life together, the answer must lie in two of the words at the heart of that saying of St Antony with which we started – 'life' and 'win'. To find my own life is a task I cannot undertake without the neighbour; life itself is what I find in solidarity, and not only in a sense of togetherness (talking about solidarity can easily turn into no more than this) but in that willingness to put 'on hold' the perspective I want to own and cling to and possess, so that the announcing of the gospel may happen through my presence and my words. And 'winning' is a word not about succeeding so that other people lose, but about succeeding in connecting others with life-giving reality. Together, these words challenge us to think about common life in some fairly radical ways.

What if the real criteria for a properly functioning common life, for social existence in its fullness, had to do with this business of connecting each other with life-giving reality, with the possibility of reconciliation or wholeness? What if the deepest threat to life together were standing in the way of another person's discovery of wholeness by an insistent clinging to self-justification? Our success – if we still wanted to use that not very helpful word – would be measurable only by the degree to which those around us were discovering a way to truth and life, and since we are not all that likely to know much about this simply on external grounds, we might never know anything at all about our success. We'd only know the struggle and weakness out of which we attempted to speak to each other; beyond that, who knows? We could be confident only in God's unfailing presence with us for forgiveness and in God's unceasing summons to us to act for the reconciliation of others.

So a properly functioning human group, doing what human groups under God are meant to do, would be one where we were engaged in learning quite intensively about the pressures that make us run away from the task God sets us. We should need to be developing some very well-tuned antennae for the varieties of competitiveness that take us over and for the ways in which we assume, secretly or openly, that success is always about someone else's loss. This prompts some uncomfortable thoughts about the sorts of disagreement we are so used to in the church. Inevitably, we think in terms of winning and losing, of this or that controversy which must be resolved in accordance with God's will so that we prevail in God's name. It isn't that the desert tradition knows nothing of controversy, of course; these documents come to us from an age compared with which many of our squabbles are pretty tea-partyish. It is simply that they leave us with the question of whether any particular victory in the constant and supposedly invigorating life of debate leaves some people more deeply alienated from God – and the nastier question of what we are going to do about it if that is so.

The church is a community that exists because something has happened which makes the entire process of self-justification irrelevant. God's truth and God's mercy have appeared in concrete form in Jesus and, in his death and resurrection, have worked the transformation that only God can perform and told us what only God can tell us: that he has already dealt with the dreaded consequences of our failure, so that we need not labour anxiously to save ourselves and put ourselves right with God. The church's aim is to be a community that demonstrates this decisive transformation as really experienceable. One of the chief sources of the anxiety from which the gospel delivers us is the need to protect my picture of myself as right and good. So one of the most obvious characteristics of the church ought to be a willingness to abandon anything like competitive virtue (or competitive suffering or competitive victimage, competitive tolerance or competitive intolerance or whatever). The church points to the all-sufficiency of Christ when it is full of people whose concern is not to separate others from the hope of reconciliation and life by their fears and obsessions. A healthy church is one in which we seek to stay connected with God by seeking to connect others with God; one in which we 'win God' by converting one another, and we convert one another by our truthful awareness of frailty. And a church that is living in such a way is the only church that will have anything *different* to say to the world; how deeply depressing if all the church offered were new and better ways to succeed at the expense of others, reinstating the scapegoat mechanisms that the cross of Christ should have exploded once and for all.[18]

The desert monastics have very little to say about theories of the atonement – apparently very little to say even about Jesus for quite a lot of the time. But they are speaking about and living out something that only begins to make sense in the context of the gospel – and we *are* reminded, occasionally but just often enough, of what they actually read and thought about each day, as we see in the story of Macarius and Theopemptus quoted above. At the centre of practically all they have to say is Christ's own command not to be afraid. Dying to the neighbour, refusing to judge, the freedom to ask, like Abba Joseph, 'Who am I?' – all this is about freedom from fear.

The desert community tells the church, then and

now, that its job is to be a fearless community, and it shows us some of the habits we need to develop in order to become fearless – habits of self-awareness and attention to each other, grounded in the pervasive awareness of God that comes from constant exposure to God in Bible reading and prayer. Put it in this way and we ought to be able to see why it is a total misreading of the desert literature to think that it's all about tolerance and niceness. Not judging anyone sounds at first like a very contemporary thing, the non-judgmental attitude that so well fits a postmodern reluctance to identify any absolute rights and wrongs, truths and falsehoods. But the desert is about the struggle for truth or it is nothing. 'God will forgive; that's his job,' said the famous eighteenth-century cynic. The desert fathers and mothers are no less sure that God will forgive, but they know with equal certainty that for us to *receive* that forgiveness in such a way that our lives will be changed is a lifetime's work requiring the most relentless monitoring of our selfish and lazy habits of thinking and reacting.

We have to be strenuous yet relaxed. Well, we might say, we know how to talk about being strenuous, how to portray Christian life as a struggle, a drama, in which we're called to heroic achievement and endurance, and we know how to talk about being relaxed, relying on God's mercy when we fail and not taking things too seriously. But it's far from easy to see how we can hold the two together. We can imagine the tightly strung pitch of effort or the slackness of relaxation, but how are both possible at once?

The desert teachers encourage us in many ways to expect the worst of ourselves. From Antony onwards, they tell us that we must expect trials to the very end,[19] and even that the apparent end of a trial or a fantasy or a distraction is a dangerous thing.[20] We need to be aware of our fragility and never stop weeping for it. Another frequent type of story in the literature is of a younger monk saying to an elder, in effect, 'Haven't you earned your passage to heaven by now? Your asceticism is so great, your penance so ardent, your wisdom so obvious.' And the older man will reply, 'If I had three lifetimes, I still couldn't shed enough tears for my sins.'[21] In the well-known treatise of St John Climacus of Mount Sinai, we read things about the need for penance that can freeze the blood of a liberal modern believer. What is hard for us to grasp is that they know with utter seriousness the cost to them of their sin and selfishness and vanity, yet know that God will heal and accept. That they know the latter doesn't in any way diminish the intensity with which they know the former; and their knowledge of the former is what gives them their almost shocking tenderness towards other sinners.

They are not, in their tears and penances, trying to make up their debt to God. They know as well as any Christian that this is paid once and for all by the mercy that arrives in advance of all our repentance. They simply want to be sure that this assurance of mercy does not make them deceive themselves about why mercy is needed, by themselves and others. If they continue with this awareness of the sinful and needy self, it is so that they will understand the tears and self-hatred of others and know how to bring them to Christ by their unqualified acceptance and gentleness. So the strenuousness is in the effort to keep before our eyes the truth of our condition; the relaxedness is in the knowledge of a mercy that cannot ever be exhausted. It could be summed up in the formula of a great Anglican monastic reformer of the nineteenth century, R.M. Benson, who believed he should have 'a heart of stone towards myself, a heart of flesh towards others, a heart of flame towards God'; though we should be careful not to take the 'heart of stone towards myself' as meaning some kind of passionate self-loathing rather than the merciless honesty which is what Benson, like the desert teachers, has in mind.

The truth is that we shall only understand the balance of severity and confidence, of the strenuous and the relaxed, in the context of the common life. Every believer must have an urgent concern for the relation of the neighbour to Christ, a desire and willingness to be the means by which Christ's relation with the neighbour becomes actual and transforming. But that urgent concern arises from the sense in *myself* of the cost and grief involved in separation from life in God, the self-awareness of frailties and failures that I cannot overcome for and by myself. I have, by God's grace, learned as a member of the Christian community what is the nature of God's mercy, which does not leave me to overcome my sin by my own effort; so I have something to say to the fellow-sufferer who does not know where to look for hope. And what I have to say depends utterly on my willingness not to let go of that awareness of myself that reminds me where I start each day – not as a finished saint but as a needy person still struggling to grow.

Sin, I said earlier, is healed by solidarity, by identification. Its power is shattered by the act of God in Christ; that act creates the community of Christ's Body in which we live, ultimately, only through each other. This helps too to make sense of the varying attitudes of the desert monks and nuns to physical self-denial. The literature has examples of real extremes of asceticism, while it has instances, some already quoted, of very relaxed attitudes to penance and discouragement of excessive zeal. Different people need different disciplines to keep them attentive: the disaster is when one kind of discipline is either practised as a means of superiority or imposed on others without attention. The whole purpose of any kind of ascesis is to challenge and overcome in ourselves whatever makes us an obstacle to the connection between God and the neighbour. So we should expect variety and should beware of any pressure to uniform severity, but the implication is also that we should beware of any slackening of the underlying watchfulness in regard to the self and its delusions. Not for nothing does the word *nepsis*, watchfulness, become the key concept of later monasticism in the Christian East.[22] If we trivialize the depth of our human need for God, we shall never be instruments to others of reconciliation. If we are unaware in ourselves of this need, because we have no disciplines for recognizing who and what we are, the church becomes ineffective.

Some of the most interesting recent research on desert monasticism has been on the significance and understanding of common life among the first generations of monks.[23] As we shall see later on, the surface pattern of 'running' or 'fleeing' from human contact is in fact a much more nuanced affair than it seems. What is to be learned in the desert is clearly not some individual technique for communing with the divine, but the business of becoming a means of reconciliation and healing for the neighbour. You 'flee' to the desert not to escape neighbours but to grasp more fully what the neighbour is – the way to life for you, to the degree that you put yourself at their disposal in connecting them with God. The unusual community that is the desert monastery of the first generation is not meant to be an alternative to human solidarity but a radical version of it that questions the priorities of community in other contexts. And this remains the most important function of any monastic community today – for the church and the wider world alike.

Something has already been said about the inevitable variety of practices in the desert communities, and this prompts a final consideration which will provide a bit of a bridge to the subject matter of the next chapter. The figures we have begun to meet in the desert are not a set of interchangeable monastic clones but highly distinctive personalities. The ideal of finding your life by putting yourself at the service of another person's reconciliation with God could conceivably be taken as a recommendation simply to stop having a self in the ordinary sense. Of course, this is a misreading, but you can see why it might look plausible. Here we have to be reminded of why the desert monks and nuns valued self-awareness. To be a real agent for God to connect with the neighbour in the way we have been thinking about, each of us needs to know the specific truth about himself or herself; that is to say, it's no good just saying to yourself, 'I'm a sinner,' in general terms. The specific facts of your experience may or may not be helpful to another – you should not assume that you always need to share the detail, but you need to know it yourself. To be the means of reconciliation for another within the Body of Christ, you must be consciously yourself, knowing a bit about what has made you who you are, what your typical problems and brick walls are, what your gifts are.

One other necessary clarification: this doesn't mean that every Christian has to have the same kind of self-consciousness – that would be to destroy the whole point. People know themselves in very diverse ways and express that self-knowledge very differently. A child may be the means of connecting a person with God, as may an adult with severe

39

learning difficulties; God forbid that holiness is the preserve of literary and educated self-awareness. But for anyone at all, even the child, even the person with a 'disability', the capacity to have some kind of loving and truthful look at yourself is surely part of the human presence that is there, to be aware somehow, at some level, of your distinctiveness, and to be aware of it as being in the hands of God. Who knows how exactly this is a reality for some human beings whose awareness is so different from what most of us take for granted? But I suspect that those who have lived their Christian lives in such company will know what I mean.

The neighbour is our life; to bring connectedness with God to the neighbour is bound up with our own connection with God. The neighbour is our death, communicating to us the death sentence on our attempts to settle who we are in our own terms and to cling to what we reckon are our achievements. 'Death is at work in us and life in you,' as St Paul says (2 Corinthians 4:12), anticipating the themes of the desert. He is writing about the whole business of how the apostle's suffering and struggle make the life of Christ visible in such a way that others are revived in hope. And it is as others discover life that we receive it too – the gift we could not have expected as we, with such difficulty and reluctance and intermittent resentment, got used to letting go of our own lives and learning how to attend in love to the neighbour. We love with God when and only when we are the conduit for God's reconciling presence with the person next to us. It is as we connect the other with the source of life that we come to stand in the place of life, the place cleared and occupied for us by Christ.

Silence and Honey Cakes

'In one of them sat Abba Arsenius and the Holy Spirit of God in complete silence. And in the other boat was Abba Moses, with the angels of God: they were all eating honey cakes.'

Spiritual tourism did not take long to develop in fourth- and fifth-century Egypt. Travellers would come from far to see one or other of the 'great old men', and the literature has no shortage of stories about some of the surprises they encountered. It is one of the most memorable of these stories that gives its title to this chapter and this book.

A certain brother came to see Abba Arsenius at Scetis. He arrived at the church and asked the clergy if he could go and visit Abba Arsenius. 'Have a bite to eat,' they said, 'before you go to see him.' 'No,' he replied, 'I shan't eat anything until I have met him.' Arsenius's cell was a long way off, so they sent a brother along with him. They knocked on the door, went in and greeted the old man, then sat down; nothing was said. The brother from the church said, 'I'll leave you now; pray for me.' But the visitor didn't feel at ease with the old man and said, 'I'm coming with you.' So off they went together. Then the visitor said, 'Will you take me to see Abba Moses, the one who used to be a highwayman?' When they arrived, Abba Moses welcomed them happily and enjoyed himself thoroughly with them until they left.

The brother who had escorted the visitor said to him, 'Well, I've taken you to see the foreigner and the Egyptian; which do you like better?' 'The Egyptian [Moses] for me!' he said. One of the fathers overheard this and prayed to God saying, 'Lord, explain this to me. For your sake one of these men runs from human company and for your sake the other receives

*them with open arms.' Their two large boats floating on the
river were shown to him. In one of them sat Abba Arsenius and
the Holy Spirit of God in complete silence. And in the other
boat was Abba Moses, with the angels of God: they were all
eating honey cakes.*[1]

What could put more clearly the sense of the distinctiveness
of vocations? This is why inattention is such a problem in the
context of the desert communities, insensitivity to the real
differences in people's callings and giftings. Silence and
honey cakes are not competing achievements to be marked
out of ten. Such anxiety as there is in the story belongs with
the visitor who can't quite cope with Arsenius's austerity (as
many other stories indicate, he was notorious for his
silences)[2] – and with the eavesdropping monk who can't see
how to reconcile the two styles; there is no hint that Moses
or Arsenius lost any sleep over their diversity.

Something of the same appears in a brief anecdote
associated with Antony himself (though it also crops up in
other contexts):

*It was revealed to Abba Antony in the desert that there was a
person living in the city who was spiritually his equal. He was
a physician; whatever he had beyond what he needed he gave
to the poor, and every day he sang the Trisagion [the threefold
liturgical prayer, 'Holy God, holy and strong, holy and immortal,
have mercy on us'] with the angels.*[3]

Some more elaborate versions begin with a 'great old man',
variously identified, actually asking God if there is anyone
who is as holy as he is, and being taken in the Spirit to
Alexandria to see some very ordinary person doing a very

ordinary job. There is no notion of a vocation that is superior in the abstract; only the attempt to identify those who become holy by doing what they alone are called by God to do. There are no standardized forms of holiness, no holiness that is impersonal. It is axiomatic that each person brings something different of the enterprise of desert life. Sin is always sin; but people live with different degrees of pressure and temptation.

A brother asked one of the fathers, 'Are you defiled by having wicked thoughts?' There was a discussion about this, and some said 'Yes' and others 'No'... The brother went to a very experienced old man and asked him about what was being discussed. The old man said, 'What is required of each person is regulated according to their capacity.'[4]

No one knows for sure how hard temptation might bear on another. It is like Augustine exclaiming in exasperated compassion, when faced with Pelagian teachers who insisted that all sin was a fully conscious rejection of God, 'most sins are committed by people weeping and groaning.'[5] A temptation that might seem trivial to you could be crushing to another; an obsession that haunts you day and night may be incomprehensible to someone else. This is why it is dangerous to demand that everyone be the same kind of ascetic; everyone comes from a different past, with different memories and abilities. We hear about a monk who complained that Abba Arsenius was not renowned for physical asceticism; the old man dealing with this asks the complainant what he had done before becoming a monk. He had worked as a shepherd, sleeping on the ground, eating sparse meals of gruel; Arsenius had been tutor to the imperial family and slept between sheets of silk. In other words, the simplicity of desert life represented no very great change for the censorious observer, but a different world for Arsenius.[6]

As already noted, Arsenius was famous not for physical self-denial but for silence; and if there is one virtue pretty universally recommended in the desert, it is this. Silence somehow reaches to the root of our human problem, it seems. You can lead a life of heroic labour and self-denial at the external level, refusing the comforts of food and sleep; but if you have not silence – to paraphrase St Paul, it will profit you nothing. There is a saying around in the literature[7] describing Satan or the devils in general as the greatest of ascetics: the devil does not sleep or eat – but this does not make him holy. He is still imprisoned in that fundamental lie which is evil. And our normal habits of speech so readily reinforce that imprisonment. Again and again, the desert teachers point out where speech can lead us astray. One of the rare occasions when something positive is said about the great but controversial monastic theologian Evagrius in the *Sayings of the Desert Fathers* is when he is depicted (not without some satisfaction) as accepting humbly the rebuke of another monk and keeping silence in a debate.[8] Abba Pambo is represented as refusing to speak to the visiting Archbishop of Alexandria. 'If he is not edified by my silence, he will not be edified by my speech,' says the old man, unanswerably;[9] archbishops are regarded with healthy suspicion in most of this literature. Our words help to strengthen the illusions with which we surround, protect and comfort ourselves; without silence, we shan't get any closer to knowing who we are before God.

So once again, we have to be careful about the risk of

modernizing the desert tradition in a shallow way. It sounds wonderful when we are told that the path of asceticism is all about self-discovery, because most of us are deeply in love with the idea of self-expression – and discovering the 'true self' so as to express it more fully is the burden of hundreds of self-help books – but for the desert monks and nuns, the quest for truth can be frightening, and they know how many strategies we devise to keep ourselves away from the real thing. As we have already seen, they are familiar with the idea that to discover ourselves all we really need is for other people to go away – or at least to fall into the parts we have written for them and not try to change us or interfere with our plans; and the essentially corporate character of monastic self-discovery is something we have seen to be fundamental to the therapy they exercise. Our life is with the neighbour. And if everybody else were indeed taken away, we would not actually have a clue about who we 'really' were. The sense in which we also need to be independent of the judgments of others is of course equally significant; but we'll come back to that in the next chapter.

As so often, it can help to take an apparently unrelated example to clarify this. The American writer, Annie Dillard, one of the most exhilarating and fresh writers about the natural world and human experience in the last few decades, has a short book on *The Writing Life*,[10] which provides a very candid and funny account of the process of creative writing. She is totally honest about the hundred and one ways in which we try to avoid the actual horrible business of writing when we have set aside time for it, and she identifies too how work in progress 'goes wild' if we leave it overnight, so that we don't know how to start again.[11] We are afraid to carry on because we know – if we are really trying to write properly – that honest self-expression is the hardest thing in the world; it needs self-scrutiny and self-abandonment.

The part you must jettison is not only the best-written part; it is also, oddly, that part which was to have been the very point.[12]

What you thought mattered – i.e. what you thought was truest to the Real You – turns out to be empty and dishonest. You have to keep asking and keep looking; no wonder we hate it and find every excuse for not getting on with it. There is a faint echo of T.S. Eliot's 'What you thought you came for/is only a shell, a husk of meaning'; or Rilke's 'archaic statue' in his poem of that name, telling you that there are no places to hide and 'you must change your life'. Your surface ideas have to go; and so does the notion that you can produce something by an act of will. I remember a sculptor of some distinction once saying to a group of students, rather to their shock, that your *will* had no part in the creative process. The use of the will is simply to keep you at it – but it doesn't deliver the product, because you don't yet know what you most truthfully want.

Some of this is put startlingly in a saying of John the Dwarf:

We have put aside the easy burden, which is self-accusation, and weighed ourselves down with the heavy one, self-justification.[13]

Very counter-intuitive, but entirely in tune with what is being said about the self in general. Self-justification is the heavy burden, because there is no end to carrying it; there will always be some new situation where we need to establish our position, dig the trench for the ego to defend. But how on earth can we say that self-accusation is a light burden? We have to remember the fundamental principle of letting go of our fear. Self-accusation, honesty about our failings, is a light burden because whatever we have to face in ourselves, however painful is the recognition, however hard it is to feel at times that we have to start all over again, we know that the burden is already known and accepted by God's mercy. We do not have to create, sustain and save ourselves; God has done, is doing and will do all. We have only to be still, as Moses says to the people of Israel on the shore of the Red Sea (Exodus 14:14).

The old joke says that the Englishman takes pride in being a self-made man, thereby relieving God of a fearful responsibility. The urge to be creators of ourselves, though, is not restricted to any one nation or class; whenever we give over our energies to self-justification, we set our feet on this road to the impossible. No wonder John the Dwarf calls it the heavier burden. We fear the other kind of burden because carrying it means that certain things are decisively out of our control and we can only respond in trust or faith. Jesus says in Matthew 11:30 that his yoke is easy – and the saying of John the Dwarf is undoubtedly meant to call this text to mind – but we can hardly forget that he also tells us to pick up and carry the cross. To see – to feel – the cross as a light load is the impossible possibility of faith: letting our best-loved pictures of ourselves and our achievements die, trying to live without the protections we are used to, *feels* like hell, most of the time. But the real hell is never to be able to rest from the labours of self-defence. It is only very slowly indeed that we come to see why the bearing of the cross is a deliverance, not a sentence; why the desert fathers and mothers could combine relentless penance with confidence and compassion.

There is a saying ascribed to Isidore the Priest warning that 'of all evil suggestions, the most terrible is the prompting to follow your own heart.'[14] Once again, the modern reader will be taken aback. 'Follow what your heart says' is part of the standard popular wisdom of our day, like 'following the dream'; are we being told to suspect our deepest emotions and longings, when surely we have learned that we have to listen to what's deepest in us and accept and nurture our real feelings? But the desert monastics would reply that, left to ourselves, the search for what the heart prompts is like peeling an onion; we are not going to arrive at a pure and simple set of inclinations. In the matter of self-examination as in others, 'the truth is rarely pure and never simple'. The desert means a stepping back from the great system of collusive fantasy in which I try to decide who I am, sometimes to persuade you to tell me who I am (in accord of course with my preferences), sometimes to use God as a reinforcement for my picture of myself and so on and on. The 'burden' of self-accusation, the suspicion of what the heart prompts, this is not about an inhuman austerity or self-hatred but about the need for us all to be coaxed into honesty by the confidence that God can forgive and heal. Henri de Lubac, one of the most outstanding Roman Catholic theologians of the twentieth century, put it with a clarity and brevity very hard to improve upon: 'It is not sincerity, it is truth which frees us... To seek sincerity above all things is perhaps, at bottom, not to want to be transformed.'[15] A few pages earlier, he has observed that 'psychology alone is not suited, at least in the most subtle cases, to discern the difference between the authentic and the sham'.[16] Like the desert teachers, he warns us against easy assumptions about the natural wisdom of the human heart.

God alone will tell me who I 'really' am, and he will do so only in the lifelong process of bringing my thoughts and longings into his presence without fear and deception. The central importance in desert practice of 'manifesting thoughts' to an elder is only partly about receiving good advice, getting problems sorted out; it is more deeply about how the elder 'stands in' for a truth that is greater than any human presence. The novice's fugues and chains of fantasy or obsession are poured out, sometimes receiving only the barest of acknowledgments and very little we would think of as counselling; but the job has been done, because the novice has been learning not to 'follow' the heart in the sense of taking what he discovers inside himself for granted, but to see the heart in all its complex, yearning, frightened actuality and to find words for it. When there is no manifestation of thoughts, there is no progress, as so many of the narratives make plain: 'Nothing makes the enemy happier,' says John the Dwarf, 'than those who do not manifest their thoughts.'[17]

Defencelessness before the elder who represents God – that is the key to growth for the monks and nuns of the desert. It is not simply a matter of submitting to the authority of an elder to be told what to do; when the novice approaches the elder and says, in the usual formula, 'Give me a word,' he or she is not asking for either a command or a solution, but for a communication that can be received as a stimulus to grow into fuller life. It is never a theoretical matter, and the elders are scathing about those who want simply something to discuss.[18] 'The desert produced healers, not thinkers,' in the fine formulation of Fr John Chryssavgis.[19] The novice, in approaching the elder, both to manifest thoughts and to ask for a saving word, is becoming vulnerable; and that is the heart of the transformation which, as Fr de Lubac says, we are by no means sure we really want, if that is what it costs.

Once again, we can think of what the church would be like if it were indeed a community not only where each saw his or her vocation as primarily to put the neighbour in touch with God, but where it was possible to engage each other in this kind of quest for the truth of oneself, without fear, without the expectation of being despised or condemned for not having a standard or acceptable spiritual life. It would need there to be some very fearless people around. A church without some quite demanding forms of long-term spiritual discipline – whether in traditional monastic life or not – is a frustrating place to live.

It is also a deeply ineffective witness to the society around. Some of the themes we have been thinking about in this chapter bear quite directly on the hidden and not-so-hidden crises of our civilization. We live in a society that is at once deeply individualist and deeply conformist; the desert fathers and mothers manage to be neither, and they suggest to us that the church's calling likewise is to avoid both these pitfalls. Think for a moment about this paradox of individualism and conformity. We are fascinated by the power of the individual will and intensely committed to maximizing this power, the power to shape and to define a person's life through the greatest possible number of available choices. In a rather odd way, as the political philosopher Raymond Plant recently noted,[20] religion (of a certain kind) can be quite acceptable in such an environment because it represents another choice that consumers can make in shaping their lives; it enriches the range of the market. The religious person in this context might well reverse what Jesus says to his friends in the Gospel of St John: 'We have chosen *you*, so that we may have the life we desire.'

And the problem is that we are actually so naïve about choices, forgetting that this world of maximal choice is heavily managed and manipulated. The rebellious teenager has a ready-made identity to step into, professionally serviced by all those manufacturers who have decided what a rebellious teenager should look like; advertising standardizes our dreams. Our choices are constantly channelled into conformist patterns, and when we try to escape, there are often standard routes provided by the very same market – 'Don't be like the crowd!' says the advertisement which is trying to persuade you to do the same as all the other customers it's targeting.

The longing for individuality, the pressure to conform; the fascination with the will and the reduction of the will to choices in the market: these are some of the knottiest tangles in our contemporary world. And to understand them fully, perhaps we need a bit more theology than we usually think about. The Russian Orthodox writer, Vladimir Lossky, based much of his theology around the controversial claim that we need to distinguish with absolute clarity between the individual and the person:[21] the person is what is utterly unique, irreducible to a formula, made what it is by the unique intersection of the relationships in which it's involved (and this is obviously grounded in what we believe about the 'persons' of the Holy Trinity, about the way God is personal); but the individual is just *this* rather than *that* example of human nature, something essentially abstract. It can be spoken of in generalities (in clichés, you might say): it is one possible instance among others of the way general human capacities or desires or instincts operate.

So the exercise of choice in the usual modern sense belongs with this natural, individual order of being rather than with the truly personal. I choose *this*: that is one way of exercising a capacity common to all, one expression of human wanting. The fact of having choices is a fact about human nature as we experience it, but it is not this that constitutes us as persons. We may like to think that the choices we make are the distinctive thing about us, what tells us and others who we are, but as Lossky (and other Eastern Christian writers of recent decades)[22] sees it, these may be some of the least distinctive, even the least interesting things, about us. We might even say that the mature human being is not the one who has the most choices available, but the one who apparently makes fewest choices, who freely does what he or she *is*, without self-consciousness or self-assertion, without anxious fretting about what would be more authentic.

We can only really make sense of this, as expounded by Lossky and his followers, if we think about the supremely free and supremely distinctive human being, Jesus. There was a certain amount of argument historically about the character and extent of Jesus' free will as a human being: could he, under the great pressure of Gethsemane, for example, have decided to escape, to do something else? If the answer is no, how can we say that he was really 'tempted as we are'? If the answer is yes, does that not make nonsense of our belief that in every moment his human nature was fully and unequivocally united with God? Not long after the age of the first desert fathers and mothers, the Eastern church was violently divided over the question of whether we should say that Jesus had one will or two: did there exist in Jesus both a divine will and a human one, or only one will that was some sort of compound of the two? The latter option assumed that if there was only one *person* in Jesus (as the official formulæ said), there must be only one will. But after a long and bitter struggle, the church decided that we should speak of two wills, because there are two natures in Christ.

It sounds appallingly abstruse to us, but in fact it is of the greatest relevance to the issues we are thinking about. To have a 'will', for the Orthodox theologians of that era, was to have a set of dispositions that went with your nature: if this is the kind of being you are, this is the *kind* of thing you're likely to want. Choosing among the kinds of thing you're liable to want is on this account a 'natural' activity. So, for Jesus in the Garden of Gethsemane, the human will is active, and the human will, like all human wills, wants to survive and rebels against the threat of not surviving. It can envisage the threat of death and what might be needed to escape death. In a purely formal and abstract sense, it is able to 'choose' to survive, because that is what human wills do.

But the human will is not the human person, and all this is quite abstract when considered apart from the person who activates the willing. There are no such things as wills that drift around in mid-air making decisions (although there are modern writers, from certain kinds of novelist to certain kinds of psychologist, who seem to suggest that this would be nice). Persons do the deciding; and when you have a person who is wholly self-consistent, whose identity is completely bound up with the calling to live in unreserved intimacy with God as Father, there is, as we say, no choice. Not because something external limits what's possible, but because the person has such solid reality, such distinctive and reliable identity, that it will do what is consistent with being *that person* – and in the case of Jesus, this means doing what God requires for the salvation of the world. There may be turmoil at the level of feelings, a keen awareness of the cost, a shrinking from what is ahead, but there is no ultimate uncertainty. And this does not mean that Jesus is somehow spared the awfulness of human decision in the face of terrible risk and agony, only that who he is is what settles the matter once and for all. He is completely free to be himself. As a matter of fact, it is unthinkable that he should refuse his calling – it is only abstractly possible in so much as any human being can, in the abstract, say yes or no to anything. But this does not reduce his freedom; instead it establishes what is the most important freedom of all.

As it happens – and it is an intriguing subject to pursue – the monastic theologians of the sixth century showed a good deal of interest in comparing the temptations of Jesus with other human temptations as part of the process of getting clear how far a sense of the possibility of doing wrong already involved some kind of mental sin. For Jesus to have suffered real human temptation, he must have gone through some of the same mental processes as we do; and if he could be tempted, yet not be held guilty, there must be some level in our minds and hearts where we can say that we are aware of the possibility, even the attractive possibility, of wrongdoing, yet not be involved in a conscious refusal of God. The technicalities of doctrine about Christ turn out to have a direct pastoral relevance for those who are tormented by guilt about what they cannot help. There comes a point where we deliberately welcome the image of wrongdoing and begin to put flesh on it in our imaginations, and that is when responsibility begins.[23] So we are encouraged to see Jesus as fully aware of the general possibilities of human nature, including the possibilities of betrayal, cowardice and self-gratification, aware of those as part of his composition as a person with a human nature, yet not actively welcoming, not saying yes to them, so that it still makes sense to describe him as without sin.

Perhaps part of the problem is that modern Western readers in particular are a bit inclined to romanticize struggle and tension. At least since Kant in the eighteenth century, there is a feeling that *really* good deeds are the ones we do with the most effort, after the biggest struggles; so our moral thinking has concentrated on the difficulties of decision-making more than on the character that develops over a lifetime. But if we think of those people whose moral and spiritual integrity has mattered to us and made a difference to us, we shall normally find that they are the ones whose behaviour doesn't draw attention to how difficult it all is, how hard they're working to be good; they are people for whom, to some extent, there is a 'naturalness' about what they do. They have become a particular kind of *person*; and that personal reality has begun to change the human nature they live in and to make slightly different things seem the obvious focus of desire. Once again, some of the theology of the Orthodox Church gives us a clue: Jesus, because as a person he is one with the Word of God, in perfect communion with the Father, changes human nature by his personal loving surrender to God in every detail of his life and death. Those who live in him by grace are in the process of having *their* human nature changed as their personal relation with him develops; they are growing into what is always fully present and accomplished in him. Human nature as transformed by his divine freedom is becoming, as we might say, 'second nature' to them.

So the saint isn't someone who makes us think, 'That looks hard; that's a heroic achievement of will' – with the inevitable accompanying thought, 'That's too hard for me' – but someone who makes us think, 'How astonishing! Human lives can be like that, behaviour like that can look quite natural' – with perhaps the thought, 'How can I find what they have found?' The lives of holy people are full of incidents that make it startlingly clear how extraordinary behaviour can arise in situations of extreme pressure without any apparent effort. John Fisher, bishop of Rochester, was to be executed for his refusal to approve Henry VIII's policies; he was woken up on the morning of his execution to be told that the time for his beheading had been changed to a couple of hours later, and he responded by saying that in that case he would welcome the chance to go back to sleep for a bit. A few years later, the Protestant martyr John Bradford was asked on the morning of *his* execution whether he felt frightened or disturbed, and he replied that he had slept so soundly that he hadn't heard the noisy singing that he was told had gone on in the cell next door. More recently, there is the story of St Edith Stein, Carmelite sister and convert from Judaism, when the Gestapo caught up with her in Holland; greeted by the officer in charge with the usual '*Heil Hitler!*' she simply replied with the old monastic formula of greeting, '*Laudetur Jesus Christus,*' 'Jesus Christ be praised.'

These are all examples of what Lossky means by *personal* action; these are memorable, distinctive – even quirky – reactions to situations, coming from people who are being wholly themselves but seem to have no individualist agenda. Thinking about them, we may come to see more clearly how to distinguish the personal from the merely individual, and to see why this is the kind of distinction we need if we are to understand fully what the desert fathers and mothers have to say about vocation and holiness. This helps us also to see once more that the desert literature has some significant things to say to us about the kind of community the church is or could be or should be. A community of mere individuals is hardly a community at all: it's a place where egos are jostling for advantage, competing for much the same goods, held together by a reluctantly accepted set of rules to limit the damage. But a community of people who had all been educated into complete conformity, so that everyone wanted what they were told to want and everyone marched in step, would have its own problems; we should be always watching one another to check for unanimity, always conscious of being policed. Plenty of societies have been down this road in the course of the last century.

The church is meant to be supremely a community of persons in the sense we've been thinking about. It is a place for distinctive vocations to be discovered in such a way that they are a source of mutual enrichment and delight, not threat. It is a place where real human difference is nourished. I don't just mean the obvious fact that the church has to be a place of welcome for all races and cultures, but that it must know how to work with the grain of different personal gifts and histories. A healthy church is one where there is evident diversity in this respect, with plenty of bizarre characters. The same thing has often been said about monastic communities, even if sometimes through gritted teeth. An unhealthy one is a group in which the unity of the church has been reduced to a homogeneity of opinions and habits, so that certain styles of devotion, for example, or certain expressions of what God means to this or that person are frowned on, virtue becomes identified with uncontroversial ordinariness and there is a nervous cultural 'sameness' in the way people talk, dress and so on. Beware of thinking this is a problem just of the right or of the left or, in general, of 'them' rather than us...

Arsenius and Moses represent irreducible differences of 'tone' in their response to the call of God in the desert, but the attitude of the tradition which conserved this story is, in effect, to ask, 'Why is this a problem?' I used the word 'tone', and it's often the case that the musical metaphor best captures what this implies for the life of the Christian community. Different voices, different instruments, but an intelligible and beautiful result. What has always to be remembered, though (and I make no apology for returning to this point), is that this is more than 'letting a thousand flowers bloom'. A church that is simply recognizing different *preferences* is stuck at the level of individualism; the real work has not yet been done, the work which is the discovery of God's call beyond the simplistic 'listening to the heart' that we all too readily settle for. This is a work which takes protracted, committed time, which is why the church is so much involved in blessing lifelong commitments – marriage, ordination, monastic life – not as a way of saying that everyone has to be involved in one or more of these but to remind all baptized believers that, because of their baptism, they are bound to the patient, long-term discovery of what grace will do with them. And it is a work that requires the kind of vulnerability to each other that can only come with the building up of trust over time, and the kind of silence that brings our fantasy identities to judgment; 'life and death with the neighbour', once more.

If the church can manage this rather difficult agenda, it will be what it should be – a powerful challenge to all kinds of human togetherness that seek to override the reality of the person, whether the subtle pressures of consumerism or the open tyranny of totalitarianism. It will also challenge some of our impulses to take a short cut around the processes of real personal exchange – whether it is the seductive idea that we can save money in education by having fewer teachers and more computers, or, more seriously, the ease with which we can learn to redescribe civilian casualties in war as 'collateral damage'. The church may not have – does not normally have – detailed solutions to practical problems in such areas, but it has a right and duty to remind the society around of what is at risk in any such short cuts.

In this light, what is an honest 'spiritual life'? Perhaps we should say that it is one in which the taste for truth (rather than sincerity) has become inescapable. We don't know what we shall be, what face God will show to us in the mirror he holds up for us on the last day, but we can continue to question our own (and other people's) strange preference for the heavy burden of self-justification, or self-creation, and weep for our reluctance to become persons and to be transfigured by the personal communion opened for us by Jesus.

3

Fleeing

'It was said of Abba Theodore of Pherme that the three things he believed to be basic for everything were poverty, asceticism and flight.'

The theme of 'fleeing' recurs many times in the desert literature, and at first sight it seems a fairly obvious way of speaking about the sheer physical separation involved in going off to the desert. As we have already seen, though, things are a little more complicated. One of the primary traditions about Arsenius tells us about a divine voice instructing him when he is still 'in the world', 'Flee from human company and you will be saved,'[2] but a probably slightly later story attached to the name of Macarius[3] suggests that the early generations of monks were well aware of the different levels at which this sort of language could be used.

Abba Isaiah asked Abba Macarius to give him a word. The old man said, 'Flee from human company.' Abba Isaiah said, 'But what does it mean to flee from human company?' The old man said, 'It means sitting in your cell and weeping for your sins.'

Certainly the desert monks and nuns are in flight from the social systems of their day, from the conformity and religious mediocrity of what they find elsewhere. But they are clearly not running away from responsibility or from relationships; everything we have so far been considering underlines that they are entering into a more serious level of responsibility for themselves and others and that their relationships are essential to the understanding of their vocation. Flight, as this saying of Macarius suggests, is about denying yourself the luxury of solving your problems by running away literally or physically from them (sitting in your cell) and about taking responsibility for your sins (weeping). We might compare the saying of Antony to Poemen,[4] that 'the great work for anyone is to go on taking the blame for their own sins before God and to expect trials till their last breath'. To solve the stress by *not* fleeing, by resorting to 'human company', is to blur the sharp edges of responsibility and to imagine that you can arrange your situation to your comfort. Change the furniture, change the scenery and you can change your inner landscape; talk to others and manipulate their reaction to you, and you can soften or share out the guilt you feel and fear. Someone has offended or hurt me, accused me of something, pointed out something I'd rather not recognize; the attractive way through is to talk to someone else and get them to reassure me that I'm wonderful and (ideally) that my critic is not worth listening to. But this is as useful in the long term as drinking salt water; I shall have to work very hard indeed at silencing the critical voice, and it can become an obsessive search for absolution. The heavy burden of self-justification again; so, say the desert fathers, *flee*: run from the company that will make you feel better but will equally involve you in a lifetime's frustration.

If we were really trying to put this in contemporary jargon, we might say that we are being encouraged to flee from 'projection' – from other people's projections onto us, ours onto them, our own inflated expectations of ourselves. In fact, if you look up 'flight' in an index of the desert fathers, you'll find quite a variety of things to flee from; and all of them have something to do with what we might think of as projection. We must flee from 'thoughts' – *logismoi* in Greek, a technical term in monastic literature for the chains of obsessional fantasy that can take over our inner life[5] – and from status and dignity,[6] and from speech.[7] 'Don't take pleasure in human conversation,' says Macarius, very austerely, as it seems to us,[8] but, as we shall see, fleeing from words is something very central indeed to all this.

Of course this is closely tied in with the themes of the earlier chapters. Your life is with your neighbour and so you must withdraw from everything that helps to imprison the neighbour, which entails looking very hard at what you say to or about the neighbour. The vocation of each is personal and distinctive, so each must have the room to grow as God, not you, would have them do. Fleeing is keeping that critical edge in awareness of what you say, keeping that reverent distance from the intimate places of the other's heart or conscience. And one very specific form of 'flight' which gives much food for thought and which comes up in a number of stories is to do with other people's conviction about what you could and should usefully do for the church: ordination is frequently presented as a burden and temptation that has to be avoided. When John Cassian famously advised monks to flee from women and bishops,[9] he had in mind the most obvious danger of being in proximity to a bishop – you might end up getting ordained. Occasionally, a desert monk was ordained against his will or his better judgment: Theodore of Pherme was made a deacon, but constantly avoided exercising his ministry, when necessary by running away.

Time after time, the old men brought him back to Scetis saying, 'Do not abandon your role as a deacon.' Abba Theodore said to them, 'Let me pray to God so that he may tell me for sure whether I ought to function publicly as a deacon in the liturgy.' This is how he prayed to God: 'If it is your will that I should stand in this place, make me sure of it.' A pillar of fire appeared to him, stretching from earth to heaven, and a voice said, 'If you can become like this pillar of fire, go and be a deacon.' So he decided against it. He went to church, and the brothers bowed to him and said, 'If you don't want to be a deacon, at least administer the chalice.' But he refused and said, 'If you do not leave me alone, I shall leave here for good.' So they left him in peace.[10]

The instant temptation is to say that figures like this were avoiding responsibility, or setting impossibly high standards to justify their refusal of office. But a better reaction would be to think first about why exactly ordination was seen by them in so negative a way. Theodore sees it in terms of the fiery pillar uniting earth and heaven, and we might recall the powerful story of Abba Joseph, raising his hands to heaven and the fingers streaming with fire.[11] The monk's calling is to 'become fire'. What then is Theodore's problem? I suspect that it is the *identification* of this personal summons to 'become fire' with a specific visible role in the church – as if ordination involved some sort of attempt to lay hold of a destiny that would take a lifetime of prayer and watchfulness to grow into. For Theodore, to be a deacon would mean to lay claim to a spiritual wholeness which it would be impossibly arrogant to assume for yourself. It's true that the church does not encourage us to understand every struggle over vocation to ordained ministry in such terms, but it is a story that ought to make all ordained people uncomfortable, if only in its clear suggestion that exercising a public role in the church's worship involves standing in the furnace of divine action which unites earth and heaven. If we can't see that this is a dangerous place, we have missed something essential.

Much of the suspicion shown towards ordained ministry, though, is rather less complex – and it applies to many more people than just those wrestling with the possibilities of ordination (which also suggests that there may be those other than bishops who can equally well be the carriers of dangerous opportunities). It has to do, certainly, with status, and so with expectation (projection once again); as for Theodore, the ordained person may be at risk because of the spiritually intense nature of the place where they must stand, but they are also at risk from the more prosaic, but still spiritually damaging, effects of hierarchy and deference. And while some Christians are of course called to exercise public ministry (the desert literature is never anti-sacramental or even anti-institutional in the sense of trying to reinvent the church as a community of perfect souls who are too spiritual to need the ordinary means of grace), the fact is that the calling to monastic witness is not going to be easily compatible with a life in which it is easy to be ensnared in the fantasies of others and caught up in an illusory position of dignity. As I have intimated, this is not by any means a problem restricted to ordained ministry – it's about any position where I have a clearly defined chance of 'doing good' and earning reputation and respect. The issue is not about whether or not someone should assume their 'proper' responsibilities in the church (or society, for that matter); the primary responsibility in the desert is, as we have seen, responsibility for your own and each other's growth and truthfulness before God.

But I wonder too whether the ambivalence about ordained ministry has something to do with the licence that the ordained person has to *talk* – to instruct, explain, exhort, even control. We have seen how wary the desert teachers could be about professional theologians and thinkers, and there are plenty of stories about the need to avoid both theoretical discussions and over-confidence on theological questions.[12] The ordained person as professional talker would hardly be likely to commend themselves in such an environment. Fleeing from speech is presented sometimes as the very climax of all flight, as in a story of Macarius:

One day, as Abba Macarius was dismissing the gathering, he said to the brothers at Scetis, 'Flee, brethren!' One of the old men asked him, 'Where could we flee to that is further away than this desert?' Macarius put his finger to his lips and said, 'Flee that.' And off he went to his cell, shut the door and sat down.[13]

It is a nicely vivid picture – the slightly jaded old monk looking around the miles of sand and asking where there is left to run to, and Macarius's immediate and eloquently simple gesture in reply. However physically remote we may be from the more obvious temptations, there is always the damage that can be done by speech, by the giving and receiving of doubtfully truthful perspectives, the half-hidden power-games of our talking – including our talking (and writing) about spiritual matters. Speech that is not centred upon the processes we have been examining – the painful confrontation of inner confusion, the painstaking making space for each other before God – is part of that system which, in another of Macarius's sayings, makes us do stupid things,[14] the world which does not know itself for what it is.

G.K. Chesterton, in his hymn 'O God of earth and altar', wrote of the 'easy speeches / That comfort cruel men', and we could say that the concern of the desert monks and nuns is to save us from easy speeches and from the ultimate cruelty they encode, the destructiveness of the lies we tell ourselves and each other about humanity. Remember Annie Dillard's observation that the bit we have to discard in our writing is what we think is best – which is often what most easily fits our expectations. If we leave this without criticism, the process of writing will not have changed us as it should. We need to develop a ruthless eye for hidden weaknesses, to make things difficult for ourselves as we write.

Lay out the structure you already have, X-ray it for a hairline fracture, find it, and think about it for a week or a year; solve the insoluble problem.[15]

That X-raying is very close indeed to the desert precepts about taking on the burden of self-accusation. In the desert, the insoluble problem is myself; the hairline fracture is the elusive but fatal element of self-regard, inattention to the neighbour, which threatens to leave me eternally broken and at odds with God and myself. Like the writer struggling to avoid the obvious and the easy, we run from what is offered to us by the 'easy' bits of our own soul or imagination and the easy ways of garnering approval from others. 'Why do you have to be so difficult?' people sometimes say to writers; the answer is that a lot of the time only being awkward saves you from being stupid and egotistical. Likewise, holy people are frequently difficult as well as exciting and inspiring. I don't mean simply temperamental or unpredictable – holy people can be these things too, like everyone else – it is more that they are not easily *reduced* to a formula, not easily conscripted into being reliable supporters of a cause, not good party members. They are too preoccupied with the X-rays.

The person who has heard the same challenge as the desert fathers and mothers, then, is in flight from conformity – not to secure a freedom of individual expression (we've seen how that can be one of the greatest illusions), but for the sake of a genuinely personal community. They will treasure silence not as a means of cutting themselves off from relationship but as a way of doing what T.S. Eliot (writing in the *Four Quartets* about the poet's job) described as 'purifying the dialect of the tribe' – restoring a language for this personal community that is as free as it can be from the little games of control and evasion that take up so much room in the talking of most of us. It's worth remembering that when Jesus tells his disciples most fully who he is, many find it 'a hard saying' (John 6:60); he does not give them an easy formula, but speaks so as to invite them to recognize him and to recognize their own deepest needs and their own deepest truth. He speaks in the context of a relationship in which truth can be uncovered for us, and his words are given to us to absorb and repeat so that we can speak for him to one another. Gradually – and by the gift of the Spirit – a new language will emerge for the new community of disciples: a language of great simplicity to speak to God (Abba, Father), a language full of surprises and daring images to speak to each other so as to echo what God has said (Bible and doctrine). Jesus in his ministry, his death and his resurrection, creates a human group where it ought to be hard to make 'easy speeches'.

The reference to what writers say about the process of writing reminds us that every search for truth involves some kind of 'fleeing', some kind of asceticism. Every act of imaginative creation, in science as well as art, needs silence, a wariness about what looks easy. And at a time when politics is increasingly dominated, it seems, by people's worries about appearance and presentation, about 'how it will play', where the culture of celebrity is a daily trading in illusory images, where show business reaches out tentacles in all directions, we need to know when and how to flee; bearing in mind that it is not *other people's* folly we are running from so much as our own deep-rooted propensity to be drawn in to these games. Remember Macarius's blunt summary, that the world is a place where they make you do stupid things.

One implication of this is a possible new definition of at least part of what's involved in being a person of faith today (or in any age, really): being a believer is manifest in how we talk, in what we think of language. What if we could recognize people of faith by how they spoke? By an absence of cliché, or of dehumanizing mockery or glib consolations? And what if conversion meant not just taking on a new vocabulary and new ideas but a new style of talking? The 'world' is a place where it is barely possible to speak without making things more difficult and destructive; the commonwealth of God is a place where speech is restored, in praise, in patience, in attentive speaking (which is bound up with attentive listening). This is not about any kind of despairing silence, being silent because there is nothing to say or know or because you're always going to be misunderstood. It is more of an *expectant* quiet, the quiet before the dawn, when we don't want to say anything too quickly for fear of spoiling what's uncovered for us as the light comes.

Thomas Merton (one of the many, of course, who has written about the desert fathers and mothers in recent times) was exercising a very Christian and a very monastic vocation when he wrote his essays in the sixties about the strange things that happen to language when it is used for advertising and for propaganda.[16] Monastic life above all has to be a life in which what is said is integrally part of a style and rhythm of living, a life in which silence is natural, expectant in the sense I have tried to outline and bound up with a right and creative kind of speaking, to God and each other. Some writers of the last few decades (including Merton himself in some of his work) have spoken of the way in which any and all of us can 'internalize' monasticism; perhaps one of the best ways for this is to learn how to X-ray our talking. It sounds frightening, because we think it suggests a severe and condemnatory atmosphere where we are always liable to be reported to the thought police for idle words. But the truth is that we are looking or listening here for speech that will affirm and open the way to life, for speech that can be playful and not just useful, for words that disturb and change us not because they threaten but because they 'fit' a reality we are just beginning to discern. If communities of faith took language this seriously, they would be extraordinary signs of transformation. And, while the desert tradition has nothing much to say about this directly, we ought to be thinking about some of this as we search for new words, songs and prayers for our worship. How easily this too becomes a sphere where easy speeches take over, where our words say too little, or try to say too much in the wrong key and where we end up sounding flat or pompous or both! But that is a long story, and not one with a short resolution.

Thinking about the language of worship does remind us, though, of one theological reason why language matters to Christians. In worship, we try to 'put ourselves under the Word of God', we try to bring our minds and hearts into harmony with what God has said and is saying, in Jesus and in the words of Scripture. We remember that God made all things by an act of self-communication, and when we respond to his speaking, we are searching for some way of reflecting, echoing that self-communication. But the same is true in all our relationships, not just in what happens in worship. If God has made all things by the Word, then each person and thing exists because God *is speaking* to it and in it. If we are to respond adequately, truthfully, we must listen for the word God speaks to and through each element of the creation; hence the importance of listening in expectant silence.

To borrow an image that appears in some of the ancient Hindu texts, we might think of the creative Word as spoken into the vast cavern of potential that is the first moment of created existence; from that darkness come countless echoes of the first eternal Word, the 'harmonics' hidden in that primal sound. When we rightly respond to or relate to anyone or anything, it is as if we have found the note to sing that is in harmony with the creating Word. Or, to use language more familiar in Eastern Christian thinking, each existent in the world rests upon a unique creative act of God, a unique communication from God within the infinite self-communication that is the one eternal Word; every being has at its heart its own word, its own 'logos'.[17] A truthful relation to anything is an uncovering of that word.

In a recent book on the use of music therapy with autistic children, there is a memorable description of how the therapist has to listen and react.[18] You let the child make what noise it wants to with the instruments put out on the floor, and you listen with all your attention until some kind of pattern or rhythm begins to emerge. When it does, you gradually begin to make some kind of pattern of noise yourself that echoes what the child is producing; communication begins, and something emerges that was not there before. So it is with our co-operation with and response to the Word of God: we must listen intently for the rhythm of divine life in what may at first seem to be unintelligible and gradually learn how to echo it and make sounds in union with it.

We Christians talk about 'speaking the truth in love' quite a bit; but in this context, this doesn't mean charitably telling other people exactly where they've gone wrong. It means finding a way to speak to them that resonates with the creative word working in their depths. Love is not a feeling of good will towards the neighbour, but the active search for that word – so that I can hear what God has to say to them and give to me through them and also so that I can speak to what is real in them, not what suits or interests me and my agenda. Sometimes this means that what at first looks like the 'loving' response won't quite do – and the desert literature shows some keen awareness of this at times.[19] A certain degree of hesitation in our willingness to offer the first kind of help that comes to our minds is no bad thing if it means that we end up attending to the reality of someone else – not giving in to the pressure that comes from wanting to make *myself* feel better. And that word 'hesitation' is one which the French philosopher Simone Weil put at the centre of her vision of how we should relate to each other in love:[20] we 'hesitate' as we might do on the threshold of some new territory, some unexplored interior. It is an aspect of our reverence for each other, and I think that it is an effective modern translation of quite a lot of what the desert fathers and mothers meant by 'fleeing'.

All this should make us think a bit harder about how we as Christians approach the whole business of ethics. It is quite clearly no part of the intention of the desert teachers to promote anything like 'situation ethics' – just thinking what the most loving thing would be and doing it – that would be to give way to the silliest kind of 'listening to the heart' and to invite endless delusion and disaster. But if the desert literature is right, then we all need training in listening and attending almost more than anything else. Unless we are capable of patience before each other, before the mysteriousness of each other, it is very unlikely that we shall do God's will with any kind of fullness. Without a basic education in attention, no deeply ethical behaviour is really going to be possible; we may only keep the rules and do what is technically and externally the right thing. But that 'doing the right thing' will not be grounded yet in who we are, in the *person* God wants us to become, and it may not survive stress and temptation. It may also be quite capable of existing alongside attitudes and habits dangerous to ourselves and each other; it may not bring us life with and through the neighbour. Our Christian codes of behaviour quite rightly tell us that some sorts of action are always wrong – torture or fraud, killing the innocent or the unborn, sexual violence and infidelity – but to see why that is so requires us to go back a step or two to see why this or that action is bound to speak of inattention, why this or that action makes it impossible to listen for the word in another person. Unless we can grasp something of that, our ethics will never really be integrated with our search and our prayer for holy life in community.

Christian ethics in fact is poised between two different sorts of consideration which are not easy to hold together in theory – a strong and uncompromising conviction of what sorts of behaviour appropriately honour God, God's image in human beings and God's purpose in the material creation; and an equally strong suspicion of the kind of instruction and exhortation that gives one person or set of persons control over others in a way that damages everyone. The desert literature does not offer any theoretical solution to this; rather it presents stories of people learning from each other. 'Do what you see me doing,' says the elder to the novice asking for guidance;[21] in other words, watch patiently how a Christian behaves. And this is not a claim by the elder to have arrived at perfection (any more than this is true of Paul's plea to his converts to be imitators of him as he is of Christ in 1 Corinthians 11:1); what the novice must witness is also the daily acknowledgment of failure and exposure to judgment, the daily loving *withdrawal* from a position of safe and authoritative superiority. This is what has to be learned, and perhaps it is a paradox only when written down, since the truth is that most of us know that the impulse to change your life commonly arises when someone is not ordering you to do so but is presenting to you, as a gift, the possibility of living otherwise. (Remember again that the holy person is the one who does *not* make you think first of all, 'That looks really hard.')

Our Christian speaking, then, arises out of 'fleeing', running from what makes us feel smug and in control, what gratifies our longing for approval and respect. In silence, as Abba Bessarion observes, you have no chance to compare yourself with others[22] – and we have seen how the tradition discourages any kind of comparison, with even the great Antony being brought down to earth by discovering who his equal in the spirit is. It is not that talking is evil or that it necessarily cheapens the truth. After all, if God himself communicates and does so in human terms, in the life and speech of Jesus, in the witness of Scripture, there must be talking that is wonderful, revelatory, transfiguring, that takes us into the heart of things. When we have found the word or phrase that anchors us in prayer, the mantra that stills and focuses us, we are discovering something of the grace and power of real language which attunes us to God's communication in a relation that is somehow both speaking and silence. It is simply that for most of the time we do not take language seriously enough. We haven't understood Jesus' warning that we shall be called to account for every word we waste (Matthew 12:36) – which presumably means every word that does not in some way contribute to the building up of myself and my neighbour as persons maturing in the life of grace. Non-wasted words may be serious or playful (we misunderstand this if we think Jesus is just telling us to be austere and businesslike in what we say), but they are all words in tune with the word God speaks in creating – which is why art and beauty and even certain sorts of humour are not alien to the work of grace. The times when we can be absolutely sure that we are wasting words are when we are reinforcing our reputation, or defending our position at someone else's expense – looking for a standard of comparison, a currency in the market of virtue.

And non-wasted words take time to mature; they must come from depth and so from the quiet and expectancy already described. At least at first, we shan't find truthful and

creative words coming easily; only those who have grown up
a bit in life with God can give the impression of speaking, not
easily in the sense of glibly, but out of an inner world in
which they are at home without self-consciousness. The rest
of us need to put some hard work into monitoring our talk.
'Just listen to yourself!' we sometimes say to a person when
we want to tell them off for careless or offensive talk; it is
excellent advice for pretty well all seasons. Language is not
an evil, but the way we so often use it means that a lot is lost
when we start talking. Here is one of the most eloquent
desert stories about this.

*They said about Abba Apollo that he had a disciple called
Isaac who was fully trained in all sorts of good actions. He had
the gift of uninterrupted prayer during the celebration of the
Eucharist. When he came to church, he did not let anyone join
him – he would say that 'everything is good in its own time, but
there is a right time for everything'. As soon as the liturgy was
over, he would flee as if he were running from a fire and hurry
back to his cell. At the end of the Eucharist it is common
practice for the brothers to be given a piece of bread and a cup
of wine; but this man would not receive these. It was not that
he wanted to turn his back on the love feast of the brethren,
but he wanted to preserve the uninterrupted prayer he had been
experiencing during the celebration of the Sacrament.*

*It so happened that he fell ill; the brothers heard about
this and came to visit him, and while they were sitting with him,
they asked, 'Abba, why do you flee from the brethren at the end
of the liturgy?' He said to them, 'I am not running away from
the brethren but from the evil tricks of the demons. If you hang
around in the open air when you're holding a lighted lamp, the
wind will make the lamp go out. We are just the same. If we*

*hang around away from our cells when we are illuminated by
the Holy Spirit, our spirit goes dark.'[23]*

It is worth recalling this when we think how deeply we prize
the visible signs of fellowship that follow most acts of
worship. The love feast is a great good – Isaac doesn't dispute
the value of the coffee and biscuits. But… something very
distinctive has happened when it feels difficult to break the
silence, when we are afraid of letting the lamp be blown out.
Even in the secular environment, we recognize this at times.
In the film *Shakespeare in Love*, the end of the first
performance of *Romeo and Juliet* is greeted initially with a
stunned silence – you can see the actors briefly wondering
whether it has been a total failure – but what has happened
is that the audience have been taken out of the 'easy' world
into another level of language and experience. The applause,
rightly, takes time to come, though when it does it is
overwhelming. And the moment of quiet at the end of a play
or concert that has moved us deeply is something we all
know. Like Isaac, we may well want to run to our cells rather
than break the moment with talk. The time may come, but
it will have *taken* time to reach the point where words
become possible. Even Isaac finds words, memorable words,
when he is challenged.

Keeping the light steady, taking the time needed for
real speech to emerge, withdrawing from the easy reaction,
the obvious phrase, the habitual and stale mode of speaking
and acting – all this implies very clearly the need for stability,
for an environment where you can indeed take the time that
is needed. Fleeing is not about constant relocation. As was
said earlier, there is all the difference in the world between
running from responsibility and 'fleeing' for the sake of truth

or honesty – that is, for the sake of responsibility. The desert tradition has a great deal to say about the temptation to think that going somewhere else will make things easier – and we shall be looking at that in the last chapter. The truth is that running and staying put are two sides of the same coin in this literature; both are about finding the way to avoid the compulsive following of your individual (not personal) agenda. What you are ultimately 'running' from is just this, your compulsions; you are making a break for freedom. So it isn't a matter of trying to run away from yourself (we'll see in the next chapter what the desert teachers have to say about these risks), but, we might almost say, running away *to* yourself, to the identity you are not allowed to recognize or nurture or grow so long as you are stuck in the habits of anxious comparison, status-seeking and chatter. As so often in these considerations, we have to think about this as a discovery of space, room to breathe. The business of living and dying with the neighbour is to do with giving someone else the room to find their connection with God; the acceptance of different callings in the name of a truly personal community is to do with making sure that my development of my own vocation isn't squeezing out someone else's. And the call to flee from privilege, safety, speech (and bishops) is a call to put some distance between yourself and the less-than-personal pressures that stunt your growth, the pressures that the Greek Christian tradition calls *pathe*, 'passions' – which is a term that is less than ideal in English for what it refers to, as we tend to assume that it means emotions in general.

The life that the desert monks and nuns speak of is a life in which there is space, but they are committed to finding that space of divine opportunity within very limited territory. The desert may look big in the photographs, but the desert as experienced is also the size of your own heart and mind and imagination, and these are not infinite spaces; indeed they may be very restricted ones. And the commitment to stay within the 'space' of these particular people's company, these daily disciplines, this unchanging environment, material and mental, is costly. It takes time, once again, to discover that the apparently generous horizon of a world in which my surface desires have free play is in fact a tighter prison than the constrained space chosen by the desert ascetics. When you have learned more or less successfully to 'flee' some of the illusory landscapes in which life appears easier, you still have to learn how to inhabit the landscape of truth as more than an occasional visitor.

4

Staying

'If you are living in a monastic community, do not go to another place: it will do you a great deal of harm.'

Although the mothers of the desert have been mentioned in these pages, their recorded sayings amount to a very small percentage of the total; they were still women in a man's world, for all that they are regarded with equal respect as far as their actual teaching goes. But perhaps it is appropriate to turn to one of them – Amma Syncletica – at this point for an image that some might think characteristically feminine:

If you are living in a monastic community, do not go to another place: it will do you a great deal of harm. If a bird abandons the eggs she has been sitting on, she prevents them hatching; and in the same way the monk or nun will grow cold and their faith will perish if they go around from one place to another.[1]

The theme is a very frequent one – suggesting that this was one of the commonest problems in the desert. A saying of Abba Moses is probably the most often quoted on this question: 'Sit in your cell and your cell will teach you everything.'[2] Learning to stay where you are becomes one of the hardest lessons of the desert, harder than apparently tougher forms of asceticism. Bearing your own company and the company of those immediately and unavoidably around you requires some very special graces, as John the Dwarf insists:

If a man has the tools God gives, he will be able to stay in his cell, even if he has none of the tools of this world. And if he has the tools of this world but lacks the tools God gives, he can still

use those tools to stay in his cell. But if he has neither God's
tools nor those of this world, it is completely impossible for him
to stay in the cell.[3]

You can cope with a certain level of demand for stability if
you have some of the resources provided by the world, some
of the skills which monastic life tries to strip you of, in fact.
But precisely because monastic life seeks to take away your
capacity to distract yourself in the usual way, by self-
dramatizing and fantasy, you have a real problem if you are
not open to God's grace. The problem is not just simple
boredom; it is what the Greek tradition refers to as *akedia*,
one of the eight great pressures on the soul identified by the
expert diagnosticians of the fifth century and later. It has to
do with frustration, helplessness, lack of motivation, the
displacement of stresses and difficulties from the inner to the
outer world, and so on. It is described classically by Evagrius
and Cassian in their writings on the 'passions'.

The morning is wearing on, getting hotter and
stickier; there is still a long time to go before eating or any
other break in the routine. Hours spent plaiting reeds for
making baskets have left you feeling numb and bored. Is
there any progress at all to be seen? Or is this life as
featureless as the sand around you? Surely making progress
would be more possible elsewhere; after all, in this dead
landscape you have no chance to share what you discover,
even if you do finally manage to discover something. And
then, this must be a selfish life: surely there's one of the
brothers who'd like a visit, who needs something? And
wouldn't I be more useful in the city, anyway? That's where
the real need is, and I could supply it so effectively!
Anywhere but here, anywhere but now…

You don't have to be a hermit to appreciate all this; anyone who lives with a routine will recognize the symptoms instantly. The fact is that we don't want to start where we are: the legendary response to the inquiry about how to get to wherever-it-is, 'I wouldn't start from here,' is exactly what we are feeling. And if, in the context of the desert and its practices and disciplines we have in some sense been brought to where we *really* are, acquainted with who we really are, it is worse, not better. The distractions are not there, the games you can play in your relations with others for psychic exercise and reassurance are forbidden (if you have been paying any attention to your spiritual guides). The ego flounders, whines, postures and pleads, and the obvious, the compelling, the practically unanswerable solution to it all is after all within your power. Change what you can: move.

Evagrius knew about it, as did all the Eastern monastic Fathers; St Benedict too, writing acidly about 'gyrovagues', monks who are constantly on the road looking for a community to suit them: anywhere but here; any colleagues but these.[4] One of the anonymous sayings also notes how we can deceive ourselves when we travel around looking for a spiritual guide who really suits us: the old man in this anecdote asks the young seeker whether he is actually looking not for an elder who can tell him what to do but for one who does what he – the 'customer' – wants: 'Is *that* what you are after to bring you peace?'[5] We are easily persuaded that the problem of growing up in the life of the spirit can be localized – outside ourselves. Somewhere else I could be nicer, holier, more balanced, more detached about criticism, more disciplined, able to sing in tune and probably thinner as well. Somewhere there is a saintly person who really understands me (and so won't make life difficult for me).

Unreality has a huge advantage over reality in some ways, since it is not obliged to obey any laws of cause and effect. But there's the catch – you are involved in those laws. So:

If a trial comes upon you in the place where you live, do not leave that place when the trial comes. Wherever you go, you will find that what you are running from is there ahead of you. So stay until the trial is over, so that if you do end up leaving, no offence will be caused, and you will not bring distress to others who live in the same neighbourhood.[6]

It is a very typical consideration that you should not be quick to move because of the message you will send to anyone in the same situation ('Don't bother; it can't be done here, with these people'). The inescapable itch and ache of living with yourself is even more vividly brought out in one of the anonymous stories:

There was once a brother in a monastery who had a rather turbulent temperament; he often became angry. So he said to himself, 'I will go and live on my own. If I have nothing to do with anyone else, I shall live in peace and my passions will be soothed.' Off he went to live in solitude in a cave. One day when he had filled his jug with water, he put it on the ground and it tipped over. So he picked it up and filled it again – and again it tipped over. He filled it a third time, put it down and over it went again. He was furious: he grabbed the jug and smashed it. Then he came to his senses and realized that he had been tricked by the devil. He said, 'Since I have been defeated, even in solitude, I'd better go back to the monastery. Conflict is to be met everywhere, but so is patience and so is the help of God.' So he got up and went back where he came from.[7]

If you find relationships difficult, what will you do about your relationship with yourself, your own body, the cussedness of ordinary things? Sin and struggle are not just about what you do to others. Conflict is to be met everywhere, not least in facing myself. So to stay in the cell is most fundamentally to stay in touch with the reality of who I am as a limited creature, as someone who is not in control of everything, whether inner or outer, as an *unfinished* being in the hands of the maker. The brother in the story has achieved an impressive level of 'spiritual' attainment, but is no less an unfinished person; what he has to learn is that his real spiritual maturity still needs the time it will take for his whole personal life to be pervaded by God and for the pressures on the soul, 'the passions', to be dealt with.

So there is a relentlessly prosaic element in the journey to holiness. Never mind the ecstasies and the feats of self-denial, never mind the heroics: the essential task is whatever is there to be done next.

A brother asked one of the old men: 'What shall I do? I'm obsessed by this nagging thought – "You can't fast and you can't work, so at least go and visit the sick, because that's a loving thing to do."' The old man recognized that the devil had been sowing his seeds and said to him, 'Go. Eat, drink, sleep, just don't leave your cell.' He was well aware that it is endurance in the cell that makes a monk what he ought to be.

For three days the brother did just this, and then he was overcome with akedia [spiritual lassitude and apathy]. But he found some little palm leaves and started trimming them. Next day he started plaiting them; when he felt hungry, he said, 'Here are some more palm leaves; I'll prepare them, and then have something to eat.' He finished them and said, 'Perhaps I'll read

*for a little bit before eating.' When he had done some reading, he
said, 'Now let's sing a few psalms and then I can eat with a
good conscience.'*

*And so by God's help he went on little by little, until he
had indeed become what he was meant to become.*[8]

Examples could be multiplied of this almost painfully
undramatic account of what you have to do to be holy. We
want something very tangible, something substantial to
mark the difference that has been made in our lives, and we
are recommended simply to get on with it, whatever
humdrum matter 'it' is. We are even warned, in this little
anecdote, to beware of looking eagerly for someone to
love – that is, using someone else to solve the problem of
your boredom and your fear of yourself. It should probably
be said that practically all of the desert elders are utterly
clear that when a specific human need presents itself, you
should respond; the point is not some abstract doctrine of
the superiority of solitude to active charity, far from it –
simply that the anxious search for an object of charity is a
bit of a giveaway. It is about *you* rather than about the
concrete call to love the neighbour.

Yet again, Annie Dillard comes to mind, describing
the ways in which we avoid getting down to the actual time-
taking work of doing what needs doing (we want to *have done*
it); and she writes that 'Appealing workplaces are to be
avoided. One wants a room with no view, so imagination can
meet memory in the dark.'[9] The staying in the cell of the
desert is likewise a 'room with no view' in this sense, a place
where the self can encounter itself. The anguish of starting
when we long to have done it already, the anguish of
confronting an inner landscape in which, when you look

honestly, there seems no hope of getting it in order, is vividly conveyed in another of the anonymous stories.

A brother fell when he was tempted, and in his distress he stopped practising his monastic rule. He really longed to take it up again, but his own misery prevented him. He would say to himself, 'When shall I be able to be holy in the way I used to be before?'

He went to see one of the old men, and told him all about himself. And when the old man learned of his distress, he said: 'There was a man who had a plot of land; but it got neglected and turned into waste ground, full of weeds and brambles. So he said to his son, "Go and weed the ground." The son went off to weed it, saw all the brambles and despaired. He said to himself, "How long will it take before I have uprooted and reclaimed all that?" So he lay down and went to sleep for several days. His father came to see how he was getting on and found he had done nothing at all. "Why have you done nothing?" he said. The son replied, "Father, when I started to look at this and saw how many weeds and brambles there were, I was so depressed that I could do nothing but lie down on the ground." His father said, "Child, just go over the surface of the plot every day and you will make some progress." So he did, and before long the whole plot was weeded. The same is true for you, brother: work just a little bit without getting discouraged, and God by his grace will re-establish you.'[10]

Reluctant gardeners will know the feeling exactly; but most of us can identify with the impulse to go to sleep for several days when faced with the sense of what needs changing in our lives. The desert elders would have understood very well the child's riddle about how you eat an elephant (a bit at a time). And the whole of their understanding of human growth and human healing assumes that trying *not* to go to sleep for several days, trying not to act as if the problem of myself will just go away or solve itself or get solved by a new environment, is the toughest challenge of 'spirituality', one which not every self-help book on spiritual growth will give us honest guidance about. The guidance we need is not so much how not to be bored, but how to face boredom without terror; not so much how to greet everything with spiritual joy and excitement, but how to preserve the quiet motivation to keep our eyes open.

One of the most telling images for this is in the advice given by another nameless elder to a brother struggling with temptation: 'Go. Sit in your cell and *give your body in pledge to the walls*.'[11] You have to *promise* yourself to yourself and to your actual environment, as if you were settling a proposal of marriage. You have to 'espouse' reality rather than unreality, the actual limits of where and who you are rather than the world of magic in which anything can happen if I want it to. The fantasy world is one in which I am not promised, espoused, to my body and my history – with all that this entails about my family, my work, my literal physical surroundings, the people I must live with, the language I must speak, and so on. It is, I suppose, a rather startling intensification of the command to love yourself in the right way. Sometimes, when Christian writers have tried to explain what it meant for Satan to revolt against God and fall from heaven, they have suggested that Satan preferred the idea of an unreal world of which he was in charge to a real world in which all glory was due to God; it is not a bad definition of the essence of evil. And it means that there is no goodness that is not bodily and realistic and local.

Is that, I wonder, the key to understanding the temptation of Jesus to worship Satan in exchange for 'all the kingdoms of the world'? It's not as though Satan owns the kingdoms of the real world so as to be able to dispose of them; all the temptations of Jesus seem to be about resorting to magic instead of working with the fabric of the real world. Jesus performs miracles in his ministry, of course, but never as a substitute for the hard material work of changing how people see God – never as a substitute for the bodily cost of love, which reaches its climax on the cross. Satan wants Jesus to join him in the world where cause and effect don't matter, the world of magic; Jesus refuses, determined to stay in the desert with its hunger and boredom, to stay in the human world with its conflict and risk. He refuses to compel and manipulate people into faith because it can only be the act of a *person*, and persons do not live in the magic world.

Indeed, we could well say that Jesus above all is literally 'a body pledged to the walls', to the limits of this world. His Body the church is 'promised' to the end of time, never defeated by Satan's forces, and that means that in this Body Jesus works with all the limitations, the fragility and the folly of the human beings he summons to be with him. He does not stop working in the church when we Christians are wicked and stupid and lazy. The church is not magic, much as we should love it to be – a realm where problems are solved instantly and special revelations answer all our questions and provide a short cut through all our conflicts. It is rather – pre-eminently and crucially – a community of persons in the sense we have already explored; so it is a place where holiness takes time and where the prose of daily faithfulness and yes, sometimes, daily boredom, has to be faced and blessed, not shunned or concealed. In the sacrament of the Eucharist we see in visible and tangible form what it means for Jesus to be pledged to this world, the Body which is always there as the community gives thanks with him and through him. Those Christian traditions accustomed to reserve the bread and wine of the sacrament and to give veneration to places where the sacrament is kept will have particularly strong associations with this idea. Some Catholic devotional manuals of an earlier generation used to speak of Christ in the reserved sacrament as 'the Prisoner of Love'; and although some now find this awkward or sentimental language, it expresses something quite central to the belief in Jesus' fidelity to the world he comes to transform. But it was the Protestant philosopher Kierkegaard[12] who put it most uncompromisingly when he said that once Jesus has accepted the human form, it was as if he could not have taken it off even if he had wanted to – an absurd way of talking, as Kierkegaard acknowledges, but it crystallizes something central, and makes us think again about what we do when we speak of Jesus as equally present in his Body and as the 'spouse' of the church, his pledged bride.

The church needs to see itself as essentially a place where 'pledging' is visible, if it is a community where Jesus' characteristic way of working is shared and shown forth. It exists in an environment in which this talk of pledging the body will sound very eccentric indeed. We are, most of us in the Western world, more physically mobile than ever; we expect change and variety in our work; we have less and less interest or commitment as a society in the ideal of sexual faithfulness; we are entertained by deliberately hectic and rapid images. It isn't difficult in this world to start imagining that the body is really a sort of tool for the will to use in getting its entertainment and satisfaction, its sense of power and fulfilment. Occasionally we are brought up short: physical illness or disability doesn't fit well with this picture; neither does really intense and selfless love; even bad weather makes us think twice about how confidently we can say we're in charge of the environment. But the pressures, 'the passions', are there in great strength, and we need disciplines to remind ourselves and each other of why the 'pledged' body is such an essential notion for human growing.

The church celebrates fidelity – it blesses marriage, the most obvious sign of the pledging of bodies. But it also blesses the vows of monastic life and solitary life, equally as signs of promise and fidelity. It lives by the regular round of worship – the daily prayer of believers, the constant celebration of the Eucharist, meeting the same potentially difficult or dull people time after time, because they are the soil of growth. It insists that we go on reading the same book and reciting the same creeds, not, we hope and pray, so as to limit and control, but to make sure that we promise to go on listening to what we believe is an inexhaustible story, a pattern of words and images given by God that we shall never come to the end of. And, quite concretely too, there is the way in which a Christian church can be a sign of fidelity, of a pledged body, in a community from which so much has fled or drained away: communities of poverty or drabness, without much to show in the way of religion or morals or culture to interest the person looking for stimulus. In very unmagical settings indeed, inner cities and prisons, and remote hamlets and struggling mission plants, the church remains pledged; its pastors and people and buildings speaking of a God who is not bored or disillusioned by what he has made – and so they speak of the personal possibilities for everyone in such a situation.

In short, a church that is faithful to its basic task is telling people that willingness to be who they are, and to begin to change only from the point of that recognition, is fundamental in the encounter with God. People can imagine that religious faith represents a deep restlessness, a dissatisfaction with the ordinary and the material; that it is poetry, not prose. They are not wrong about the poetry – but poetry has to be made out of profoundly ordinary experiences, in the words that everyone uses. Practically all the great religious traditions insist at some point that holiness involves a new encounter with the prosaic along the way to transformation. And Christianity, as I have been suggesting, has a particular theological reason for valuing the local and material: God has acted and spoken directly in the material of a human life, in the language of ordinary vulnerability. The divinity of Christ is not some 'internal' fact about him, it is what his entire human existence, soul and body, makes present (which is why in the early church, it mattered so much *not* to identify the divinity of Jesus with his mind or spirit, but to see it as pervading his entire identity).

Christianity encourages me to be faithful to the body that I am – a body that can be hurt, a body that is always living in the middle of limitations; it encourages me to accept unavoidable frustration in this material and accident-prone existence without anger. To talk about pledging the body to the walls in the sense of the fundamental decision to be where and who I am is also to open the door to the recognition carried in another of the sayings of Amma Syncletica:

There are many who live in the mountains and behave as if they were in the towns. You can be a solitary in your mind even when you live in the middle of a crowd. And you can be a solitary and still live in the middle of the crowd of your own thoughts.[13]

When external solitude is accompanied by the jostling crowd of fantasies and longings and fugues of speculation, the body is not really pledged to that solitude. But the body itself can be a hermitage when I have embraced it as quite simply the place where I know I shall meet God – the here and now of my actual humanity. And solitude becomes possible, the kind of solitude that is expressed in the 'death to the neighbour', the lack of judgment, the reticence in speech that we have observed in the desert. Grace returns us to the particular and local. Just as there are no neighbours in the abstract (neighbours we want to go and look for to satisfy our own desire to be useful), only the actual human material around us, so there is no individual soul in the abstract, only the human material of my body, my words, my memories; my gifts, my weaknesses. The lawyer in the Gospel who asked, 'Who is my neighbour?' and prompted the parable of the Good Samaritan was asking a perfectly serious question at one level, because the command to love the neighbour isn't abstract; the pity was that he needed to be shown what was under his nose. Like most of us.

Only the body saves the soul. It sounds rather shocking put like that, but the point is that the soul (whatever exactly that is) left to itself, the inner life or whatever you want to call it, is not capable of transforming itself. It needs the gifts that only the external life can deliver: the actual events of God's action in history, heard by physical ears, the actual material fact of the meeting of believers where bread and wine are shared, the actual wonderful, disagreeable, impossible, unpredictable human beings we encounter daily, in and out of the church. Only in this setting do we become holy – in a way entirely unique to each one of us.

It has been said that sanctity is inimitable. While I can think, and probably you can as well, of some very holy people who cry out for imitation because of all their quirks of behaviour, the imitability in question is not of that kind. I cannot become holy by copying another's path. Like the novice in the desert, I must watch the elders and learn the shape and the rhythm of being Christian from those who have walked further and worked harder; but then I have to take my own steps, and create a life that has never been lived before. At the Day of Judgment, as we are often reminded, the question will not be about why we failed to be someone else; I shall not be asked why I wasn't Martin Luther King or Mother Teresa, but why I wasn't Rowan Williams. The journey is always one that leads into more not less uniqueness; all to do once again with the call to be persons, not individuals.

The desert looks shapeless – the sandy desert of Egypt especially, where the sand shifts and landscapes dissolve. It looks like nowhere in particular; yet you go into it so as to become more particular than ever. In the modern context, you could compare it with the other sort of non-place we are familiar with – places stripped of any local identity, featureless and totally unsurprising – the airport lounge, the fast-food outlet, places designed entirely for individuals looking for repeatable experiences. No doubt fourth-century Alexandria had its equivalents: our job, as particular people trying to live something of a calling to contemplation, as a church looking for renewal and integrity, is to seek out the non-places where we can become personally faithful. We need to identify those bits of our immediate environment that can serve as sites for recovering a covenant with the self and the body. Like Annie Dillard writing about writing, we have to find somewhere dark enough for memory and imagination to join hands: not harsh places whose austerity is itself distracting, not comfortable ones where we can drift away from the here and now, but simply places to settle and make friends with myself before God. This is as much true for our daily prayers as for retreats or longer-term commitments. You can, as Amma Syncletica says, be alone anywhere, but learning that may need some very well-thought-out strategies along the way.

So we come back to the beginning: our life and death is with the neighbour, the actual here and now context in which we live – including that unique neighbour who is my own embodied self and whom I must confront truthfully as I confront all the rest truthfully. Holiness doesn't begin tomorrow or over there or with that person, not this; it doesn't begin with that church, not this. One of the implications of what we have been thinking about is that we need to recognize the dangers of looking for the ideal church community (full of people like me), and to ask how I 'pledge my body' to the Christian community I am actually with. Of course there are crises that can lead to tragic separation, of course God leads us at times into new settings; but for a very great deal of the time our difficulties are not to do with these questions of fundamental integrity but with the ordinary stresses of living with other equally unsatisfactory Christians. If you leave a church community too quickly, you find it becomes a habit; more salt water to drink. Sooner or later you will have to confront the challenge of being pledged to uncomfortable reality – and of how to cope with that inner restlessness which constantly suggests what look like simpler solutions, avoiding the difficult route of changing myself.

Many Christian churches now refer to those periods of the liturgical year when no great festivals or fasts are unfolding as 'Ordinary Time'. It is a telling phrase; inevitably *most* of the time in the year is 'ordinary' – yet all of it is the time won for us by Jesus Christ, all of it is gift, and in that sense extraordinary. It can never be strictly ordinary time, since it is the time in which day by day we are brought into the story, the drama, of God's action in Jesus. And the secret of living through the liturgical year lies in remembering the extraordinariness of the time that simply unfolds day after day, because it is the time in which we are constantly called and enabled to move and grow, in whatever circumstances face us. Here we are daily, not necessarily attractive and saintly people, along with other not very attractive and saintly people, managing the plain prose of our everyday service, deciding daily to recognize the prose of ourselves and each other as material for something unimaginably greater – the Kingdom of God, the glory of the saints, reconciliation and wonder. And we embody our decisions in both prayer and relation, inseparably, giving to both the attention they claim, so that together we begin to know ourselves found by God.

A monk's cell is like the furnace in Babylon where the three young men found the Son of God. And it is like the pillar of cloud where God spoke to Moses.[14]

There is the rationale of staying in the cell, pledging the body and pledging to the body. Where we are and who we are is the furnace where the Son of God walks. When we begin to discover what contemplative faithfulness means, we recognize that we are in that furnace; very, very occasionally, around an unexpected corner or with an unexpected person, we catch a glimpse of the fire, the desert filled with flame.

Questions and Answers

We print below the question and answer session that concluded the John Main Seminar led by Rowan Williams in 2001.

How much do we actually know about the 'desert mothers'?

Not a great deal, but a number of names survive with sayings and stories attached – such as Amma Syncletica, whom I quoted. They seem to have lived in communities of their own; there is not much suggestion in the literature that they were invariably under the direction of male ascetics – rather the contrary. And that is a mixed blessing from the historical perspective, as it means that women are largely absent from the narrative traditions of the male groups. Yet figures like Syncletica were obviously taken very seriously by the male tradition.

At the beginning of the fourth century, Methodius of Olympus, who taught in Asia Minor, wrote an important dialogue set in a community of women; and in this dialogue female figures were given the role of expounding aspects of the Bible and the life of prayer and asceticism. Although it's written by a man, it suggests that women were expected to know about such things, and even expected to be listened to. Then later in the fourth century, we have St Macrina, sister of the two great Cappadocian fathers, Basil and Gregory of Nyssa. Gregory wrote a life of his sister, and also a dialogue *On the Soul and the Resurrection*, which depicts him visiting Macrina on her deathbed and conducting a very sophisticated dialogue on the inner life and the nature of desire. It's very notable that throughout Gregory refers to Macrina as 'the teacher'. So it is not entirely a man's world in the fourth-century desert – though there is the persistent notion that a woman who takes part in this way in the ascetical life is a sort of honorary male.

Can you say more about the difference between person and individual?

I am basing myself largely, as I said, on the work of the Russian theologian, Vladimir Lossky. Although there are other writers who do something similar with these ideas, he is one of those who gives fullest definition to the distinction and does so in the context of reflecting on the doctrines of God and Christ. For him, 'person' is always the mysterious uniqueness that defies any definition. What makes me myself is ultimately something for which there are no words. There simply is this singularity, this place no one else can occupy. But only in relationship can you see this. So the realm of the personal is that realm in which what I am, unique, mysterious and distinctive, comes into relation with what is unique, mysterious and distinctive in you. Each of us then makes the other yet more unique and mysterious and distinctive in the process of encounter.

For Lossky it is very important that the church be a community of persons. There are, he says, two errors into which people may fall here. The church can be a community of individuals, people who are making a concordat, a compromise with each other to live together: 'We don't really know quite how much we have in common, but we'll manage somehow.' For Lossky (I don't necessarily endorse this) this is the error of Protestantism – drawing up an agreement so that we can cope. But the opposite error is to treat the church as a solid mass, undifferentiated, insensitive to the distinctiveness of each – the error of Catholicism, in his eyes. Unsurprisingly, he sees Orthodoxy as having the balance right.

The essential difference between individual and person is that the individual will always be an example of a type, an instance of a generality. I pick up an object, a glass, say, and identify it as an individual case of the type; there are lots of glasses, but they are variations on a single theme, examples of a general substance or nature. They are different from each other, but always with the same things in common. Lossky insists that when we talk of a person we talk of what is infinitely more than an instance of a type. A person in Christ, a person becoming holy, is most particularly more than an 'example' of something, their meaning, we might say, coming from something less special or unique than themselves. The meaning is in the utterly one-off character of their relation with the person Jesus Christ.

Individuals are repeatable and thus in some ways replaceable; persons aren't. Do you remember the end of the song 'Clementine'? 'So I kissed her little sister, and forgot my Clementine': that's exactly what personal relation is *not*. No little sisters will do. Drop the glass on the floor and you'll find another to do the same job; break a relationship and there is no simple substitute. For every person there is one way in which they can show God, and only they can do it like that. So the life of God is reflected in the whole set of distinct Christian histories, distinct responses to and creative engagements in the world. I enjoy telling people at Confirmation services that when I ask the Holy Spirit to come into their lives in this sacrament, it becomes true that there is then something they can do in their community that no one else can – which means that the church needs them as they need the church.

If the heart is the place where the love of God takes root, where is the danger in being guided by the heart?

Confusing on the surface, perhaps, but there is a logic behind it. When Abba Isidore expresses his warnings about being guided by the heart, he is warning us against listening to what we *think* are 'deep' promptings. 'How can I be wrong if I'm so sincere?' is a poor guide for the Christian.

On the other hand, of course, if we can get to the true depth of the heart, what is there is the echo of God's creative Word; as I suggested, each creature is a sort of echo of God. It's not that if we got to the centre of ourselves, we'd find the Ten Commandments inscribed there, but that there is a natural orientation to God on our very being, our humanity, and our task as we grow in grace is to recover our 'attunement'.

But we have so jarred the harmonies, we are so compulsively and habitually out of tune, that we hear only what is out of tune, the self-protection and self-regard that buries the echo of God in the heart. If listening to the heart means only listening to a deeper selfishness, forget it; that would be only to canonize what we think is going on in us. There is work to be done before we can really listen to the hidden music.

How do we discern the will of God?

Someone once asked the great Anglican monastic theologian Herbert Kelly this question: 'How do we know what the will of God is?' He famously answered, 'We don't. That's the joke.' Tempting to leave it at that, really.

Kelly is right: we never know absolutely precisely, incontrovertibly, what the will of God is in specific complicated circumstances. I can recall wrestling with a particularly serious pastoral problem in the diocese, not knowing at all what to do, and saying to God at the end of Evening Prayer one day, 'Just for once, couldn't you consider telling me… ?' But I know it doesn't work like that, though it's what we all think we want.

So what does discernment look like? I have to choose between a number of courses of action: well, what course of action more fully seems to resonate with the kind of life Christ lived and lives? What course of action opens up more possibilities for God to 'come through'? These are not questions that will immediately yield an answer, but they are the raw material of reflection. What course of action might be slightly more 'in tune'? What opens rather than closes the doors for God's healing and reconciling and creating and forgiving work to go on? There's no guarantee that in any situation there will be only one clear and compelling answer to such questions. But, if these are the questions we're asking, the very process of reflecting and discerning is making space in ourselves for the life of Christ and the creative movement of God. To the extent that we truthfully and sincerely make that space, we are already in tune a little bit better with God; so even if we go on to make a mistake, we shall have done something to leave open the door to God in the decision we made. And so we shall have moved some way towards doing God's will by leaving God some room and freedom to salvage our lives from whatever mess our decisions may bring with them.

Why is there a connection between winning the brother and winning God?

Winning the brother or sister isn't – in the perspective of St Antony – a matter of getting them signed up to something, getting them on your side, but opening doors for them to God's healing. If you open such doors, you 'win' God, because you become a place where God 'happens' for someone else, where God comes to life for someone in a new and life-giving way – not because you are good and wonderful but because you have allowed the wonder and goodness of God to appear (and you may have no idea how). When we shift our preoccupations, anxiety and selfishness out of the way and some space appears for God, we ourselves are brought more in touch with God's healing. And so, in winning the brother or sister, we win God.

What are the links between John Main and the desert fathers?

One of the essential teachings I have taken from Fr John and the tradition he represents is the importance of a particular kind of stability in prayer, a faithfulness in the practice. That's why I'd connect John Main's teaching with the courage to go on 'staying' in the cell or wherever. The emphasis on the mantra and the persistent discipline of going on with it makes perfect sense in the context of the kind of life the desert teachers are talking about – a life where we are always trying to put aside our self-preoccupation and self-dramatizing, our compulsion to be in charge.

More specifically, of course, the very idea of meditating in this way stems from the desert tradition. John Cassian, who was so important to John Main, was a monastic writer who flourished in the fifth century and made it his life's work to digest and summarize the wisdom of the great desert figures, in a series of 'interviews' with the 'great old men'. He and his companions visited the monastic heartlands of Egypt, asking one of the fathers after another for their wisdom and noting their replies. Cassian turns these into lengthy and more polished discourses. Here we find the notion of prayer focused on the repetition of formulae that still the mind. But the same thing is echoed in other works from the same period or a bit later, in the Palestinian, Sinaite and Syrian writings, especially those that introduce the classic eastern formula of the Jesus Prayer ('Lord Jesus Christ, Son of God, have mercy on me, a sinner') – the form used with the eastern 'rosary'.

Since it is from this desert world that the traditions of meditation we share derive, it can be very important for people today who seek to meditate as Christians to understand something of the desert and how these practices of prayer fitted into it.

Who are the equivalents of the desert monks today?

There are still many who inhabit deserts of one sort or another. In the last century there have been those who have gone off on their own or have been taken into their own form of desert, and so have become for others a touchstone of Christian integrity. You may think of Charles de Foucauld and the Little Brothers of Jesus exploring their Christian calling in a literal and physical desert and in the desert of the anonymous urban environment. Then there are other great figures like Thomas Merton and Bede Griffiths. They speak from the desert because they – in a sense – make themselves homeless by putting themselves on the edge of the life of the conventional church and its habits. Both started out as safe Catholic converts and good monks; as they went on, they became rather more shaky Catholics in the eyes of many and very unusual monks. They became familiar with a desert landscape in which the external points of orientation were elusive; they had to find another kind of map. So too with Henri le Saux, Abhishiktananda, a conventional Belgian Benedictine who went to India to find that the landscape of his life and faith was dissolving, to be reconstituted at a deep level.

But I think also of Dietrich Bonhoeffer in the desert of his death cell, where he produced such amazing reflection; his letters are among the greatest spiritual testaments of the century. Think of his wonderful letter in May 1944 written on his godson's christening, in which he writes of how easy it is for our religious words to become empty, how we have to discover again how they can be transforming for a whole world. His desert had taught him that the old words were still there – but stale, tired, rubbed down, so much that we no longer knew how they could have their content restored, so that all we could do was to betake ourselves to prayer and action for justice, and say as little as possible.

Some have lived on the edges of things for the sake of the Kingdom, while others have combined action and contemplation in transfiguring ways – such as Desmond Tutu. So we look for the deserts today and their 'monks' in the marginal places of world and church; we listen carefully for what is said there, and what is not said. We are not devoid of desert fathers and mothers.

In what way is silence authenticating?

The quality of our silence is a real issue. There is a silence that is poisonous and evil – when someone is being silenced by someone else; a silence that is resentful, because it is the bottling up of feelings that I can't trust myself to express and can't trust anyone else to listen to; then there is the silence that is attentive, focused, coming out of peace not anger, coming from fullness not woundedness (well, perhaps from both…). Our freedom to be silent in this latter way is the index of our freedom from resentment and from the struggle for power. That's why authentic silence is difficult; yet it indicates an affirmation, a great Yes to life in freedom.

My wife and I have often talked about the Simon and Garfunkel song from the sixties, 'The Sound of Silence': in that song, silence is a terrible thing ('Silence like a cancer grows'), malignant and destructive, because it is about people being silenced, about words falling away into helplessness so that falsity and idolatry take over. And just that is the exact opposite of the silence we are thinking about. We need to know how to tell the difference.

And in conversation, or in a teaching or a pastoral relationship, we need to know also how to 'read' silences. There can be a silence that indicates 'I am giving up here; I don't know how to relate or respond; I feel useless'. My greatest pastoral mistakes have been when I sense that I have silenced someone, made them feel that they can't speak, feel overwhelmed, disempowered. There can be silence in a teaching relationship that says, 'You seem to know all the answers, why should I bother to say anything.' (And it can come from either side of that relationship!) We need such discernment, because despite these dangers, there are silences in these contexts that are right and good. And alongside my memories of pastoral disaster, I can also remember times when I knew I needed to say nothing and neither did the other person, and it was evidently a right silence.

Where is the church going?

I strongly believe that the promise of Christ that the church will not fail is one we can trust. This is for the simple reason that the church is above all the community of those whom Jesus calls to receive the Spirit and to share the relation he has to his Father, to the eternal Source. Because Jesus doesn't stop issuing that invitation, the church doesn't stop existing. That is the bottom line, for me.

But it also seems to me that as time passes it will be harder to think that the future of the church will have just one institutional shape across the globe or even more locally. In some areas, the church is already beginning to exist, as we might say, in parallel lines – not in sealed compartments, but in different styles and idioms, with real interchange between them. This actually puts more rather than less of a burden on those called to leadership or pastoral oversight; they have the job of 'orchestrating' these differences into something other than competition and disharmony. This is, I find, an increasingly significant part of my daily work as a bishop.

Can the institutional church teach the contemplative path?

The church is always renewed from the edges rather than the centre. There is a limit to what the institutional church can do: institutions have their own dynamic and their own problems, and renewal tends not to come from central planning (it was St Francis who went to Pope Innocent III, not the other way round). No one planned the role that Benedictine monks would have in the history of the church and Europe, and in the teaching of meditation and contemplation today.

Institutionally, the parish system works up to a point, but it is one among several ways of being a church. For many people, in addition to parochial loyalties, there are crossparochial ties and networks that feed and sustain them. What needs to happen within the parish structure and what needs to happen around all the non-parochial networks is a re-visioning of the church. Nearly all Christians have inherited a *functional* idea of what the local Christian community is for: it gathers us for sacramental worship (with the sacraments seen rather as routine duties). But I think we need to break free a bit, recognizing that, in addition to the sacraments, we meet for other kinds of togetherness, in study and prayer – which means challenging any model based on Sunday patterns alone.

Another thing, harder to express, is that those of us who have the freedom to do so need to go on asking where the unity of the church lies and in what that unity consists. I believe it is a unity which exists fundamentally in a shared gazing towards Christ and through Christ looking into the mystery of the Father (which is what the sacraments celebrate and make possible). If we believe our unity comes from that looking together into a mystery, occasionally nudging each other to say, 'Look at that!', we can perhaps recognize that the unity we enjoy is not first and foremost an institutional matter; it is the common direction in which we strive to look. Of course we must be willing to nudge each other, as I put it, and tell each other what we're seeing. I think if we began with something a bit more like that, we'd see more space in the church for the contemplative dimension. If there aren't enough people looking in to the mystery, unity comes to be seen in functional terms – meeting for events, discharging our obligations – and we miss the vital and living element of unity.

Meister Eckhart said, 'There is nothing so much like God as silence.' What does this mean?

Silence is letting what there is be what it is, and in that sense is profoundly to do with God. When we experience moments where there is nothing we can say or do that would not intrude on the integrity and beauty of what is before us, that is a silence that takes us into God.

There's a second-century Christian document known as the Protogospel of James, in which we find a description of the moment of Christ's birth. Joseph has gone off to find a midwife; Mary is still in the cave. And as Joseph is walking into the village, suddenly everything stops. Joseph himself relates how he sees a shepherd in the field dipping his bread into the pot and his hand arrested halfway to his mouth; a bird in mid-heaven halted as it flies. For a moment everything stands still, then movement begins again and Joseph knows that the birth has happened in that moment of absolute stillness.

Where is the line between sacred and profane?

Islwyn, a Welsh-language poet of the nineteenth century, said in one of his works, 'Everything is consecrated.' Sometimes we see the sacred and the profane as if they were 'territories' lying side by side. But the image I prefer is more of a layered one. At root everything is consecrated, touched by God; everything is enfolded or interwoven, as Eastern Christians might say, in the Wisdom of God. Profanity is what happens when the crust of managing and fantasy hardens over this interwoven, living reality. The profane is the sort of thing I see very plainly these days in advertising, for example: not that advertisers individually are wicked people, but the industry is a human enterprise constructed around a set of controlling, fantasizing 'profanities' or surface reactions. So a search for the sacred is not looking for holy 'territory' so much as searching for what lies beneath the surface.

How do you handle akedia?

Confession time? Yes, it strikes – most often in the form of that deep anxiety about whether, as Evagrius said, you might not be able to serve God better somewhere else; or in the 'What's it all for?' feeling when you've signed the twentieth letter of the morning and made the fourth uncomfortable phone call. You have emerged from a depressing meeting about next year's budget and there's a meeting with the investment advisers after lunch, followed by a school assembly somewhere, with the institution of a new vicar in the evening and about twenty minutes between return from one and leaving for another. It all has to be done, but *akedia* is the sense that this wasn't what I intended when I was ordained – and it's so hard to be holy in the middle of this and wouldn't it be easier if... The only solution is to let myself be drawn deeper into the present moment: making a point sometimes of looking out of the window, putting my hands on the arm of the chair, *sensing* what's there, feeling the 'fabric' of the moment and saying as I breathe, 'Here I am; this is what I am; this is what I do next; here is God.' It's the equivalent of basket-weaving in the desert. Who knows what serves God? Do what's there. God meets me in this moment and nowhere else.

In John 12, Jesus says, 'Where I am, there will my servant be also.' This must mean that where I am, trying to serve my Lord in this moment, Jesus is. So you are with Jesus at the Diocesan Board of Finance, with Jesus as you try to deal with the pastoral fallout of a clerical marriage in difficulties, with Jesus as you count to twenty at an irritating letter of angry complaint that you have just received about something you have no particular responsibility for. You have to find out what it is to be with Jesus in moments like these, because he is with you there. 'Where I am, there will my servant be also.' Opening the moment to God, letting yourself be drawn in to its depth with him – that's the only real cure for *akedia*.

What does religious education mean in our modern cultural desert?

At root the answer has to be about whether we believe religion is first about fullness of life or about duty and control. Religious education, when it is doing its job of 'educating the spirit', must be conveying, in all aspects of the educational environment, a sense of the peaceful worthwhileness of each person. Each person as he or she is at rest is worthwhile – they don't become worthwhile by all they do when not at rest. It's from that point that God will move in them, create afresh, change. My own fascination with religious education especially in the primary school is focused on the messages that are given by the whole life of the institution about peaceful worthwhileness. There are few sights so wonderful as a school hall with three or four hundred children sitting in complete silence and learning the first steps in meditation – I have seen it and it can be done! They have been told, 'You have room just to sit and breathe in God's presence.' Their worthwhileness when at rest is being affirmed. And I suspect that this sort of thing is much more fundamental in religious formation than any simple communicating of religious information.

I don't think children become mature persons of faith unless they have been helped to experience their own humanity in some such way. As a theologian, I'd say that this was a matter of being taught to experience their humanity as created, loved and healed; you may not immediately say it to them in those words, but that is the basis on which you move. The temptation is to think that religious education is about bolting on more information. But what really educates is the whole atmosphere of a school or college. Too often, the institution as a whole is pushing tense, driven messages, messages of anxiety about filling up the empty spaces and never wasting time. This can mean that the arts and music and drama, even sport, are pushed to the edges except as further forms of competition. In such an atmosphere, whatever you're *saying* about religious or spiritual matters, what you're doing is breeding atheists, because you're creating a shrunken humanity.

What would the desert fathers and mothers say to young people today?

They might say, 'What's the hurry?' They would be amazed to see the way our culture prizes speed. They might say that the hurried urgency to possess is an index of falsehood and a misunderstanding of the kind of being you are. It's all right to take time. Only in taking time can you realize how much more you are than an individual. By taking time, you are built by the character of the whole world you are in and the people around you.

What were you leaving when you became a bishop?

All sorts of things: peace and quiet, for instance! On one level, I felt I was leaving behind a sense of innocence. Not that the academic world is all that innocent, but as a bishop you have to make decisions that need to be clear and can be hard or hurtful. You are a public person in a way that means you will be misunderstood and you can't explain yourself; if you try, you are into the heavy burden of self-justification with a vengeance. Put bluntly, I think I was being asked to leave behind an environment where I could feel more pleased with myself than bishops normally can. That is one of the bittersweet gifts of this job, which you must get used to. But of course it's true for anyone in various ways. The gospel may lead you into a role where you have a life in other people's fantasies and you can't do anything about it. It can hurt and feel imprisoning, yet this is part of the price you pay for the reality you are trying to minister or mediate as a pastor. Perhaps I was being pushed into another level of understanding my priesthood in becoming a bishop – even more in becoming an archbishop.

Are you being selective about the desert fathers' teaching on the body?

Yes. Of course there are other aspects in the teaching of the desert fathers, as in the whole early Christian tradition, and some of it does have a deeply negative feel (the desert monk who said, 'My body seeks to kill me, so I kill it.'). Yet at the same time, people really were discovering in their practice the crucial importance of the body. Throughout the history of Christian asceticism, the tension goes on. The body is never, for the Christian, something neutral, nor is it ever simply evil. It is a place where struggle goes on.

What do we want our bodies to say? Asceticism is one way of saying something with your body, just as much as the pledging of the body in sexual fidelity is saying something with the body. What has been recovered by scholarship in recent decades is a sense that the surface concern of some of the early Christian fathers with asceticism conceals a sense of the immense and creative importance of the body as a way of communicating and connecting with God and the world. Of course Christianity inherits a set of mixed messages on all this, which we are still sorting out. But I have deliberately tried here to retrieve some of those elements that are most easily sidelined or ignored, trying to suggest how much of the desert wisdom can lead us in a more positive direction.

After all, we are still the 'early church' – what we call the early church is just the very early church, and we don't fully see how the church will be when it has grown more. There are all sorts of questions that arise in learning from the first teachers of the Christian desert, but they all point us to a future where both questions and answers will look different, the future of silently gazing on God.

Footnotes and Bibliography

Names followed by a number indicate that the quotation is from the Alphabetical Series; 'Anon.' with a number refers to the Anonymous Series in the translation of Benedicta Ward. The numbering and organization of the Anonymous Series in the original languages is a nightmare of complexity, given the divers streams of transmission, and it is simpler to have one scheme of reference; Ward's introduction, p. xviii, explains some of the complexities and gives the corresponding numeration in the most important Greek text.

Footnotes

Preface

1. Benedicta Ward, *The Sayings of the Desert Fathers: The Alphabetical Collection*, Oxford/Kalamazoo: A.R. Mowbray/Cistercian Publications, 1975; revised ed. 1984

2. John Chryssavgis, *In the Heart of the Desert: The Spirituality of the Desert Fathers and Mothers*, Bloomington, Indiana: World Wisdom Books, 2003.

Chapter 1

1. Antony 9; c.f. the saying ascribed to him in Athanasius's *Life of Antony* 67, which confirms the authenticity of this tradition.

2. Moses to Poemen 1.

3. Moses to Poemen 3; the implication is that without this no one can rightly see themselves as a sinner.

4. John the Dwarf 39.

5. Joseph of Panephysis 2.

6. Macarius 32.

7. Macanus 3; c.f. Macanus 21, on Macarius's reaction to the severe discipline of another abba.

8. Poemen 12; c.f. Sisoes 20 for a closely similar story.

9. Macarius 3; c.f. Poemen 62, a good example of both identification with the sinner and modification of another's harshness. Poemen

tells the questioning monk that his previous adviser has his thoughts in heaven, while 'you and I' still suffer from sexual temptation. See also Poemen 6 for a rebuke to a hermit for judging harshly.

10. Moses 2.

11. Anon. 123.

12. Bessarion 7.

13. Macarius 32.

14. Poemen 64; c.f. Anon. 186 for a slightly more complex response, but with the same concern to nurture humility.

15. Poemen 92.

16. Moses to Poemen 4 and 7; c.f. Poemen 6.

17. Poemen 118.

18. On the whole scapegoat impulse, see the work of René Girard and James Alison, especially Girard's *Things Hidden Since the Foundation of the World*, London: The Athlone Press, 1987, and Alison's *Raising Abel*, New York: Crossroad, 1996.

19. Antony 4.

20. John the Dwarf 13; c.f. Anon. 38.

21. E.g. Dioscorus 2.

22. See the sayings in Anon. 132–48. For the importance of *nepsis* in later literature, see the treatise on the subject by Hesychios the Priest (probably eighth century or a little later) included in *The Philokalia* (eds. G.E. Hions Palmer, P. Sherrard and K. Ware, vol. 1, London: Faber & Faber, 1979, pp. 162–98). The whole of *The Philokalia* is in Greek described as the work of the 'watchful' fathers.

23. See especially Graham Gould, *The Desert Fathers on Monastic Community*, Oxford: Clarendon Press, 1993, and Douglas Burton-Christie, *The Word in the Desert*, Oxford/New York: Oxford University Press, 1993, chapters 8 and 9.

Chapter 2

1. Arsenius 38.

2. Arsenius 2, 4, 25, 42.

3. Antony 24; c.f. the more obviously pious variant preserved in the Alphabetical Collection under the name of Eucharistos.

4. Anon. 84.

5. Augustine, *De natura et gratia* xxix. 33.

6. Arsenius 36.

7. E.g. Theodora 6; and c.f. Macarius 11 and 35.

8. Evagrius 7.

9. Theophilus the Archbishop 2.

10. Annie Dillard, *The Writing Life*, New York: HarperCollins, 1989.

11. Ibid. p. 52.

12. Ibid. p. 4.

13. John the Dwarf 21.

14. Isidore the Priest 9.

15. Henri de Lubac, *Paradoxes of Faith*, San Francisco: Ignatius Press, 1987, p. 127.

16. Ibid. p. 122.

17. Poemen 101.

18. Theodore of Pherme 9.

19. *In the Heart of the Desert*, p. 76.

20. Raymond Plant, *Politics, Theology and History*, Cambridge: Cambridge University Press, 2001, chapters 11 and 12.

21. Lossky's fullest exposition of these themes can be found in the posthumous collection of his essays, *In the Image and Likeness of God*, Crestwood, New York: St Vladimir's Seminary Press, 1974, especially chapters 6 and 7, and in the 'Postscript' to *Orthodox Theology: An Introduction* (again a posthumous volume edited from transcripts of lectures in Paris), St Vladimir's Seminary Press, 1978, pp. 119–37.

22. See particularly the work of Lossky's pupil, Olivier Clement, e.g. *Questions sur l'homme*, (2nd ed.) Quebec, 1987, and *La revolte de l'esprit*, Paris, 1979; and that of the Greek theologian, Christos

Yannaras, e.g. *The Freedom of Morality*, Crestwood, New York: St Vladimir's Seminary Press, 1984.

23. There are many discussions in *The Philokalia* of the phenomenology of temptation and of the sense in which Christ is truly tempted: e.g. Hesychios, 'On Watchfulness and Holiness' 46 (vol. 1, pp. 170–71) and John Damascene, 'On the Virtues and the Vices' (vol. 2, London: Faber & Faber, 1981, pp. 337–38).

Chapter 3

1. Theodore of Pherme 5.

2. Arsenius 1.

3. Macarius 27.

4. Antony 4.

5. They are discussed at length by Evagrius and Cassian; see vol. 1 of *The Philokalia*, pp. 38–52 and 73–93.

6. E.g. Cronius 5, an anecdote about a monk who had been a senior civil servant and in the desert distinguished himself by his lack of concern for his personal appearance.

7. E.g. Macarius 16.

8. Macarius 41: 'Flee from human company, stay in your cell, weep for your sins and don't take pleasure in human conversation; and then you will be saved.'

9. Cassian, *Institutes* xi. 18.

10. Theodore of Pherme 25; c.f. Isaac of the Cells 1 and Peter of Dios 1.

11. Joseph of Panephysis 7 (c.f. 6, a more prosaic version of what is obviously the same tradition).

12. Poemen 8; a visitor tries to discuss 'heavenly things' with Poemen, who responds only when the guest begins to ask advice about the passions of the soul. This echoes Poemen 62, already quoted. C.f. Antony 17, the commendation of Abba Joseph for saying, 'I don't know,' when asked about the meaning of a text.

13. Macarius 16.

14. Or 14.

15. *The Writing Life*, p. 10.

16. See, for an overview, the article on 'Language and Propaganda' in *The Thomas Merton Encyclopedia*, eds. William Shannon, Christine Bochen and Patrick O'Connell, Maryknoll, New York: Orbis Books, 2002, pp. 242–44.

17. The idea is especially important in Maximus the Confessor, and has been used in the modern period by the Romanian theologian Dumitru Staniloae; see Charles Miller, *The Gift of the World: An Introduction to the Theology of Dumitru Staniloae*, Edinburgh: T. & T. Clark, 2000, pp. 60–62.

18. Mercedes Pavlicevic, *Music Therapy: Intimate Notes*, London: Jessica Kingsley Publishers, 1999, especially pp. 20–21.

19. John the Dwarf 2, Theodore of Pherme 15, 28.

20. E.g. Simone Weil, *Intimations of Christianity Among the Ancient Greeks*, London, 1957, pp. 24–55, on power as what stands in the way of reflection, hesitation, in the presence of another person. For a fine discussion, see Peter Winch, *Simone Weil: 'The Just Balance'*, Cambridge: Cambridge University Press, 1989, pp. 107–108, 164ff.

21. E.g. Isaac of the Cells 2, Poemen 73, 174, Sisoes 45.

22. Bessarion 10.

23. Isaac the Theban 2.

Chapter 4

1. Syncletica 6.

2. Moses 6.

3. John the Dwarf 44.

4. See above, note 5 to chapter 3.

5. Rule of St Benedict, chapter 1.

6. Anon. 68.

7. Anon. 69.

8. Anon. 63; c.f. Arsenius 11 for a shorter version.

9. *The Writing Life*, p. 26.

10. Anon. 76.

11. Anon. 73.

12. Søren Kierkegaard, *Philosophical Fragments/Johannes Climacus*, ed. and tr. Howard and Edna Hong, Princeton: Princeton University Press, 1985, p. 55: 'From the hour when by the omnipotent resolution of his omnipotent love he became a servant, he has himself become captive, so to speak, in his resolution and is now obliged to continue (to go on talking loosely) whether he wants to or not.'

13. Syncletica 19.

14. Anon. 74.

Bibliography

Primary sources in translation

Ward, Benedicta, *The Sayings of the Desert Fathers: The Alphabetical Collection*, Oxford/Kalamazoo: A.R. Mowbray/Cistercian Publications, 1975; revised edition 1984

Idem., *The Wisdom of the Desert Fathers: Apophthegmata Patrum (The Anonymous Series)*, Oxford, 1975.

Significant recent studies

Burton-Christie, Douglas, *The Word in the Desert: Scripture and the Quest for Holiness in Early Christian Monasticism*, New York/Oxford: Oxford University Press, 1993.

Chryssavgis, John, *In the Heart of the Desert: The Spirituality of the Desert Fathers and Mothers*, Bloomington, Indiana: World Wisdom Books, 2003.

Gould, Graham, *The Desert Fathers on Monastic Community*, Oxford: Clarendon Press, 1993.

Ramfos, Stelios, *Like a Pelican in the Wilderness: Reflections on the Sayings of the Desert Fathers*, Brookline, Massachusetts: Holy Cross Orthodox Press, 2000.

Starowieyski, Marek, ed., *The Spirituality of Ancient Monasticism: Acts of the International Colloquium Held at Cracow-Tymic 1994*, Tymic/Cracow, 1995 (especially J. Pollok, 'The Present State of Studies on the Apophthegmata Patrum: an Outline of Samuel Rubenson's and Graham Gould's Perspectives', pp. 79–89).

Stewart, Columba, 'The Desert Fathers on Radical Honesty about the Self', *Sobornost* 12, 1990, pp. 25–39, 131–56, repr. *Vox Benedictina* 8, 1991, pp. 7–53.

Idem., *Cassian the Monk*, Oxford: Oxford University Press, 1998.

The World Community for Christian Meditation

Meditation is the missing dimension of much Christian life today. It does not exclude other types of prayer and indeed deepens reverence for the sacraments and scripture.

Laurence Freeman OSB

Meditation is a direct pilgrimage to your own centre, to your heart. To enter the simplicity of it means learning a discipline. With faith and patience, meditation leads to deeper and deeper realms of silence.

It is simple and practical. It is about experience rather than theory, a way of being rather than thinking. Because of the profound effect meditation has on one's life it is even more than a method of prayer: it is a way of life, a way of living from the deep centre of one's being in every situation.

Medio Media

MedioMedia is the publishing and communication company of The WCCM and stocks a wide range of books, audio and video material in support of those wishing to follow a more contemplative spiritual path. Visit the website www.mediomedia.com for a free catalogue or contact:

MedioMedia
St Mark's, Myddelton Square
London EC1R 1XX
Tel: 44 (0) 20 7713 7201
Fax: 44 (0) 20 7713 6346
E-mail:mediomedia@wccm.org

Meditation creates community. Since the first Christian Meditation Centre was started by John Main in 1975 a growing community of meditators has arisen around the world. The International Centre in London co-ordinates and supports this international community with a regular quarterly newsletter giving spiritual teaching and reflection. If you would like to learn more about the community and receive the newsletter and information on retreats and events such as the Annual John Main Seminar, please visit the website www.wccm.org or contact:

The World Community for Christian Meditation
International Centre
St Mark's, Myddelton Square
London EC1R 1XX
Tel: 44 (0) 20 7278 2070
E-mail: mail@wccm.org

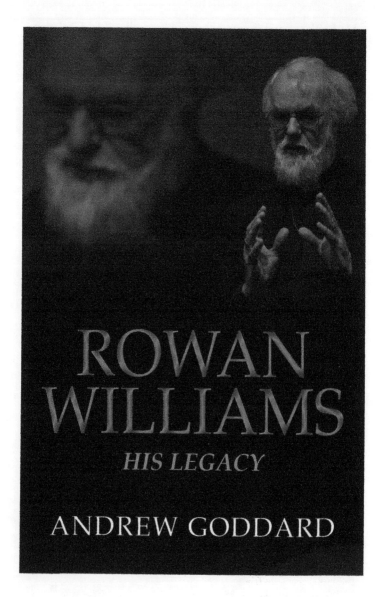

ROWAN WILLIAMS

HIS LEGACY

ANDREW GODDARD

Rowan Williams:
His Legacy

Andrew Goddard

9780745956022

Rowan Williams has served as Archbishop of Canterbury through one of the most turbulent periods in the history of global Anglicanism. How has he coped with the huge issues of a divided church and a rapidly changing world? What has he done as archbishop when parts of the church are campaigning for an "inclusive church" with gay-partnered clergy and women bishops, while others are determined to resist these developments? How has he related to other Christian traditions and those of other faiths? What has he said about the Iraq war, the financial crash, Sharia Law?

Andrew Goddard's fascinating assessment of Archbishop Rowan's time in office draws on Williams' speeches and writings, as well as interviews and comments from those close to him. This book shows the pressures faced by an academic scholar who only took on this demanding role because he believed it to be God's call.

The Revd Canon Dr Andrew Goddard is Associate Director of the Kirby Laing Institute for Christian Ethics (KLICE), and a part-time tutor in Christian Ethics at Trinity College, Bristol.

"Andrew Goddard's portrait of Rowan Williams succeeds in being fair, shrewd, lively, and many-sided. In particular, he shows with crystal clarity that Rowan has actually modelled a different, and Christlike, form of 'leadership'."
Professor Tom Wright, former Bishop of Durham

"Here in this wonderful book you are given the opportunity to see a true living saint, scholar, and servant of God."
Canon Andrew White, author of *The Vicar of Baghdad*